Coaching and Mentoring

OTHER ECONOMIST BOOKS

Guide to Analysing Companies
Guide to Business Modelling
Guide to Business Planning
Guide to Economic Indicators
Guide to the European Union
Guide to Financial Management
Guide to Financial Markets
Guide to Investment Strategy
Guide to Management Ideas and Gurus
Guide to Organisation Design
Guide to Project Management
Guide to Supply Chain Management
Numbers Guide
Style Guide

Book of Obituaries
Brands and Branding
Business Consulting
Business Miscellany
Dealing with Financial Risk
Economics
Emerging Markets
The Future of Technology
Headhunters and How to Use Them
Marketing
Mapping the Markets
Successful Strategy Execution
The City

Directors: an A–Z Guide
Economics: an A–Z Guide
Investment: an A–Z Guide
Negotiation: an A–Z Guide

Pocket World in Figures

Coaching and Mentoring

What they are and how to make the most of them

Jane Renton

THE ECONOMIST IN ASSOCIATION WITH
PROFILE BOOKS LTD

Published by Profile Books Ltd
3A Exmouth House, Pine Street, London EC1R OJH
www.profilebooks.com

Typeset in EcoType by MacGuru Ltd
info@macguru.org.uk

Printed in Great Britain by
Clays, Bungay, Suffolk

A CIP catalogue record for this book is available
from the British Library

ISBN 978 1 84668 189 9

The paper this book is printed on is certified by the © 1996 Forest Stewardship
Council A.C. (FSC). It is ancient-forest friendly. The printer holds FSC chain of
custody SGS-COC-2061

FSC
Mixed Sources
Product group from well-managed
forests and other controlled sources
Cert no. SGS-COC-2061
www.fsc.org
© 1996 Forest Stewardship Council

Contents

Introduction

Being a journalist by trade and British can make one doubly cynical. In setting out to detail the nascent coaching industry, which has to a degree overshadowed its more humble and less well-remunerated sister, mentoring, I also began to question whether coaching was all it was cracked up to be. Was it simply a feel-good device for the overpaid, overpampered executive of the boom years of the early 21st century? After a year of researching and endeavouring to define this curiously elusive industry, I am less cynical. I have met many remarkable, highly principled people who work as coaches or mentors, and whose motives I have no wish to impugn. But I am still struggling with my initial question. Perhaps it is more honest to acknowledge that the rise of coaching is largely explained by the growing complexity of our lives; by the fast pace of technological change; and the recognition that leadership in this environment is both tough and bewildering. We require additional help in a world that is often frighteningly non-collegiate. In this environment the coach is someone to watch over you, to encourage you without judgment and censure.

Coaches and mentors, as I have discovered, come from a variety of different backgrounds and disciplines. Some are simply rebadged trainers who have discovered that it is trendier – and better paid – to restyle themselves as coaches. But others, skilled in psychology or psychotherapy, have spent many years acquiring coach-specific qualifications. Some have no industry-specific qualifications at all. Some business coaches are driven by business needs and processes, while others are motivated by life's "bigger picture" and a subversive desire to reform individuals and businesses. Selecting a coach can be a hit-or-miss experience in an industry where there is still no consensus on the correct definition of coaching, or the limits of its endeavours. Clearly, research is needed to find out whether coaching really works in the long run.

This book aims to deliver a much-needed practical layman's guide. Much of the available literature on the subject is written by coaches for other coaches or would-be practitioners. Instead, I have attempted to provide the reader with some idea of where coaching sprang from by listing the psychology and business ideas that underpinned it. I have also sought to provide some guidance to anyone who plans to engage the services of either a coach or a mentor as well as outline of the some of the issues facing both coaching and mentoring. It has been no easy task, since there was no obvious beginning, middle or end, because coaching – and its poor relation mentoring – embraces so many other disciplines in other fields, such as sports and even medicine. As one coach, quoting Gertrude Stein said, "There is no there there." Coaching is a thieving magpie that has borrowed its ideas from others. Even the more ancient art of mentoring posed problems, since there is a dearth of literature surrounding the subject.

As far as coaching's origins go, I have confined myself to focusing on a handful of psychologists and gurus from business and elsewhere who coaches themselves say have influenced their nascent industry the most. Some who read this book will no doubt argue, with some justification, that others should have been included and that my selection is too American-centric. But coaching, with its essentially optimistic leanings, is largely an American construct, which will broaden and internationalise in time, which any later editions of this book will hopefully reflect.

I have met many wonderfully kind and generous people in the course of this project who provided me with ideas, research and interviews. I would like to take this opportunity to thank them for their support and involvement – they know who they are. I would particularly like to acknowledge the help I received from Vikki Brock, a former Boeing executive turned business coach, who not only allowed me to read her doctoral dissertation on coaching's origins, but also provided introductions and contacts. I also want to thank Caroline Horner, head of the i-coach academy, and mentoring experts David Clutterbuck and Julie Hay, who were similarly helpful. Since I am no psychology expert, I would like to acknowledge Tom Butler-Bowden, whose excellent books *50 Psychology Classics* and *50 Self-help Classics* provided further additional information about some of the psychologists and gurus who featured in the first two chapters of this book. Tim Hindle's *Guide to Management Ideas and Gurus* was another useful resource. I would also like to thank my publisher, Stephen Brough, at Profile Books, for giving me the opportunity to write this book as well as much-needed coaching support to chivvy me along the way.

Jane Renton
August 2009

The origins of coaching

Tell me, and I will forget.
Show me, and I may remember.
Involve me, and I will understand.

Confucius, 450 BC

The new and unregulated coaching industry derives from many different and sometimes conflicting disciplines, theories and methodologies that are both strengths and a source of confusion for those seeking its services.

It is hard to pinpoint who the world's first coach really was. It could have been some military instructor from the ancient world with a natural talent for killing and an unnatural talent for philosophy. Perhaps a more deserving recipient of that honour would be Socrates, a famous classical Greek philosopher, who possessed legendary skills in helping others achieve their goals but whose blunt speaking earned him powerful enemies and an untimely death. The father of western philosophical thought posed a series of questions, not just to solicit individual answers, but to encourage fundamental insight into the issue at hand. That most morally principled of men, Socrates said the unexamined life was not worth living. In other words an individual has to constantly challenge accepted precepts, conventions and beliefs in order to improve. It could have been lifted straight from any contemporary guide to coaching techniques. But Socrates, unlike modern coaches or the Sophists of his day, whom he attacked for their relativism, never charged a fee for his teachings. He left behind no self-help manual, no handy five-step plans – we simply have to take his student Plato's word for it that Socrates was on to something big.

Definitions

A quick scan of the etymological dictionaries sheds little light on coaching's origins other than the limited knowledge that the noun "coach" derives from a "large kind of carriage", usually of the grander variety, initially built from the mid-15th century onwards in the Hungarian town of Kocs (pronounced "coach"). The word spread throughout the rest of Europe and perhaps the only analogy that can be drawn with current executive coaches is that they helped get you from A to B, preferably in the quickest possible time, arriving the right way up and alive – no mean feat given the atrocious state of most European roads and the high levels of brigandage at the time. By the mid-19th century, the word coach began to be used as Oxford University slang for a tutor: one who carries or coaxes his student through an exam. The word also appears in the works of George Eliot, an English novelist who was a woman whose real name was Mary Anne Evans. Like the sports coach, the Oxford coach bore little resemblance to the modern version, merely instructing and imparting knowledge as would any competent teacher operating on conventional lines. The modern coach, like Socrates, asks killer questions and it is up to the client to come up with the answers and accompanying action plan.

There are many differing and sometimes conflicting interpretations of what contemporary coaching is actually about. At its most simplistic, coaching helps you to help yourself, whatever your chosen goal might be, or as Martin Lukes, a fictional anti-hero devised by *Financial Times* columnist Lucy Kellaway, puts it in Kellaway's send-up of the corporate world, *Martin Lukes: Who Moved My BlackBerry?*, "to do better than your bestest". Meanwhile, the coaching industry, struggling hard to achieve professional recognition, is hard pressed to come up with a more businesslike description, let alone a more grammatical one.

The definition put together in 2006 by Australian coaching

psychologists Anthony Grant and Michael Cavanagh is big on jargon but short on sex appeal:

> A goal-directed, results-orientated, systematic process in which one person facilitates sustained changed in another individual or group through fostering the self-directed learning and personal growth of the coachee.

The International Coach Federation, the largest of the world's professional coaching organisations, elaborates on the above, insisting that "coaches do not advise clients" and that "the client has the answers". But as a convincing "elevator pitch" – the 20-second opportunity to spell out what you do to potential clients – it somehow fails to grab, let alone explain.

Sir John Whitmore, one of coaching's early pioneers, who borrowed and then adapted the "Inner Game" sporting techniques developed by a former Harvard University tennis coach, Tim Gallwey, before bringing them to the UK, puts it more simply:

> Coaching is unlocking a person's potential to maximise their own performance. It is helping them to learn rather than teaching them.

Edgar Schein, a professor at MIT Sloan School of Management, now in his 80s and the first to coin the term "corporate culture", views coaching as essentially a subset of consultancy. He defines it as:

> A set of behaviours on the part of a coach (consultant) that helps the client develop a new way of seeing, feeling about and behaving in situations that are defined by the client as problematic.

Donald L. Kirkpatrick, a former national president of the American Society for Training and Development, describes coaching in entirely corporate terms:

> Initiated by manager; done on a regular basis; job-oriented; being positive or corrective with emphasis on telling, training and teaching by the manager; and with the objective to improve job performance.

There is also an underlying assumption that the person being coached is willing to participate in coaching and possesses the underlying abilities and talents to achieve the goal that they set for themselves, or that has been set on their behalf.

Complexity and diversity

The struggle to define coaching is largely a result of the complexity and diversity of the professional disciplines, methodologies and theories that helped shape it, many of which date back to the early 20th century and before, especially on the psychological front.

That underlying diversity can be viewed as a strength, argues Vikki Brock, an executive coach based in Ventura, California, and the nearest the fledgling coaching industry has to its own historian:

> *Coaching is a consolidation and amalgamation of many fields and the integrative thinking of great pioneers.*

But such diversity can also be something of a liability. It can mean a lack of clarity as to what professional coaching really is and what makes for an effective or reputable coach. There is already a great deal of confusion and disagreement about professional and ethical standards.

As part of her doctoral dissertation on coaching and human development, Brock endeavours to identify the root disciplines on which coaching is based. These are primarily:

- philosophy;
- psychology;
- consulting;
- education;
- management;
- mentoring;
- sports.

Her list also includes organisation development, sociology, training, the performing arts, career development and the so-called

12-step development programmes for addiction and other behavioural problems.

At the fringes are a group of mind/body therapists who can be crudely lumped together under the banner of the human potential movement. They include a wide and disparate array of practices such as:

▶ Gestalt theory – a form of psychotherapy;

▶ psychosynthesis – the connection of emotions to values and meaning;

▶ Rolfing – a form of deep tissue massage;

▶ bioenergetics – another form of body psychotherapy;

▶ the Alexander technique – a form of physical realignment;

▶ EST (Erhard Seminar Training) – large group awareness training practised by the Forum and Landmark;

▶ Silva Method (formerly Silva Mind Control) – a mixture of meditation, visualisation and positive thinking.

Nearly 45% of respondents in Brock's survey cited business as the occupation predominantly influencing the coaching industry today, with nearly 22% citing the psychology profession as the most important influence on the coaching method, while sports and education rank 10% and 8% respectively. Her findings are based on an international survey sent to 10,000 coaches, together with an extensive trawl of what has been written about coaching as well as individual interviews with over 170 coaches, many of whom helped pioneer the industry.

Early days

Coaching as a distinct discipline in its own right did not really take off until the 1990s, but early references to it began to emerge in human resources journals as far back as the mid-1930s. The first peer reviewed paper on coaching appeared in *Harvard Business Review* in 1955. At that stage coaching was seen purely in terms of supervision. Supervisors should be trained to coach staff to be more effective.

In 1930 a number of psychologists were hired by an engineering firm to study the best way of organising an office in corporate America. Some broke away in 1944 to set up a service organisation, RHR, on the premise that business leaders needed a sounding board, preferably someone who was outside their business. This RHR outsider was increasingly used to help select and recruit potential leaders and to generally bounce ideas off. At the time, RHR referred to its work as development or even counselling, but nevertheless much of its work bore striking similarities to the role undertaken by high-level executive coaches today.

Towards the end of the 1950s there was a discernible shift by clinically oriented industrial psychologists towards developmental counselling at senior management level, as it was believed that many of the operational problems experienced by businesses stemmed from senior managers' attitudes and actions.

The 1960s heralded a more optimistic, forward-looking age as well as the arrival of the humanistic movement with its belief that if you treated people well you would get much better performance from them. It was during this period that the human potential movement got under way, along with the hippie movement and anti-Vietnam war protests. It was about rejecting establishment views and seeking new forms of "enlightenment". This came in the form of the Beatles and a fusion of eastern spirituality and alternative medicine, all of which would have a considerable impact on the fledgling coaching industry. On a more mundane level, in business circles the term counselling began to be slowly replaced with the term "executive coaching", yet much of what are considered as signs of early coaching still involved psychologists going in to talk to managers on a one-to-one basis to help them with work adjustment, or to help them become less abrasive in their dealings with others. But business coaching was beginning to branch out into many of the more holistic or positive things that it does today.

There was also a growing recognition that you cannot divorce work from personal life. Richard Boyatzis, a psychologist and an expert in organisational behaviour, says:

> *If a person says to me "I keep my work and my personal life*
> *separate", I know that's a form of pathology. We've known that*
> *since pre-Freud, when people compartmentalise, they actually*
> *segment their personality. In mild forms it's dissociation. In*
> *major forms it's called psychosis. It's unhealthy.*

The term counselling never sat easily in corporate life. Counselling
was and still is associated with weakness and inadequacy. According to Bruce Peltier, a San Francisco-based clinical psychologist, the
reason that executives have coaches rather than counsellors is that
most would love to see themselves as "corporate athletes", or at
least high performers, but would baulk at the idea of entering into
therapy.

It is hardly surprising that during this era Tim Gallwey's *Inner
Game* series of books began to move out of the sporting world to
make an even greater impact in the world of business. Gallwey's
driving idea was that the opponent, or rather the negative thoughts
that resided in the human mind, was far more formidable than the
one that faced you on the other side of the tennis court. According
to Whitmore:

> *Gallwey was the first to demonstrate a simple and comprehen-*
> *sive method of coaching that could be readily applied to almost*
> *any situation.*

A growing impact

By the late 1970s and early 1980s coaching was beginning to make
a greater impact in corporate life. It was slowly being used as a
device to help managers improve performance, rather than simply
correct perceived deficiencies. In the UK it also began to be seen as
a useful device for helping colleagues learn how to solve problems
through guided discussion and activity.

It was about this time that management consultants began adopting many of the characteristics and techniques of coaching. There
are some striking similarities between the two disciplines in that
they both often address the same issues, although they involve
different emphases and approaches. In general, the most common

form of coaching focuses on asking the right questions, and the most common form of consulting focuses on solving problems by coming up with the right answers.

On a more personal level, Weight Watchers was founded on self-help and group support principles. It was and still is a hugely successful worldwide organisation and one that has had many of its tactics emulated by group coaches.

The idea of personal development also began to spread to business life. Controversial new-age guru, Werner Erhard, who set up Erhard Seminars Training (EST), joined forces with Fernando Flores, a Chilean businessman and former senator, to establish the Forum training designed to appeal more widely to the corporate world. In 1984 Erhard formed a corporate business division, Transformational Technologies, which among other things promoted coaching from a consulting perspective.

By the end of the 1980s coaching had entered the business lexicon. But it was still not seen as a distinct discipline in its own right, rather an adjunct to other activities. Managers would be offered coaching for specific tasks.

Coming of age

All that was to change in the 1990s when the coaching phenomenon became firmly established as an important management development method for senior managers in major global corporations. It seems that sweeping technological change, globalisation and all the complexity and increased competitive pressures that they entailed produced a fertile environment in which coaching could flourish. So too did rising incomes.

Workplace coaching covered just about every business aspect:

► personal careers;
► transitions and change;
► mergers and start-ups;
► entrepreneurialism and leadership;
► groups and teams.

Coaching was no longer the exclusive domain of *Fortune* 500 company boardrooms; its services were being sought by enterprises of every size and type. Brock says:

> It was about all those things and more. I think that the fascination with coaching stemmed from our yearning to replicate something that is missing from modern life. We are knowledgeable but not necessarily wise.

In other words, the pressures of growing complexity and intense competition, together with job insecurities, have made many people more fearful and anxious. This holds true especially in the higher echelons of corporate life, where coaching has found a rich client base. Life may be well-remunerated at the top, but to crudely paraphrase Thomas Hobbes, a 17th-century English philosopher, it is also nasty, brutish and short. The average tenure of a CEO in any of the FTSE 100 companies is currently around five years.

The style of top management in many companies militates against collegiality, with an unspoken taboo against admitting to any form of human vulnerability. Mark Goodridge of ER Consulting, a British firm specialising in organisation behaviour change, says:

> Coaching needs to be seen in the light of that insecurity. How long do you hold on to your job? In the hire and fire modern corporate world, the coach is someone to watch over you and someone – importantly – who is not a colleague.

This view is echoed by Peter Block, an American business guru and author of several best-selling business books, including *Flawless Consulting: A Guide to Getting Your Expertise Used* and *Stewardship: Choosing Service Over Self-Interest*:

> I think the best business leaders – and certainly the ones I work with – know that corporate life is very tough on their people and genuinely want to do something about it.

In business, the 1990s also saw a proliferation of cross-discipline approaches and theories with many new leadership theories emerging and increasingly coaching was seen as the missing link to making such theories more of a reality. Christopher McKenna, author of *The World's Newest Profession: Management Consulting in the Twentieth Century*, says:

> *Neither academic scholars nor journalists worried about the professional credentials of consultants, but instead presumed that they responded to market forces like any other occupational group.*

The same holds true for coaches, who continue to struggle for professional recognition in the same way as management consultants did before them. Part of that quest has given rise to more rigorous academic research, particularly in the area of business coaching and its impact on work performance. Twice as many articles about coaching were published between 2000 and 2004 than in the whole of the 1990s. Many of them appeared in psychology journals as well as management and training publications. Many of the new books about professional coaching showed clear links with earlier psychological underpinnings.

Many leading coaches are psychologists

Many of the world's leading coaches are psychologists by training, but according to Brock it would be wrong to assume that any company or individual seeking coaching should select only those suitably qualified in the discipline:

> *I think there's room for all in this field. A lot of US-based psychologists are moving into this area because they're finding that it's much more fun to work with healthy individuals, rather than those who are mentally unwell or depressed.*

American psychologists are also discovering that by moving into coaching they can move out of the troubled American health-care system, thus avoiding battles with insurers for payment, and into the corporate world where it has been possible to earn a lucrative living – at least until the global financial crisis sparked by the credit crunch that began in 2007.

There are essentially three schools of western psychology:

▶ the post-Freud school that essentially dwells on developing mature emotions;

▶ the cognitive-behavioural school that focuses on how external stimuli affect behaviours and how cognitive interventions can modify them;

▶ the humanistic-transpersonal school, with its more optimistic forward-leaning focus on the individual and self-advancement.

Coaching generally focuses on the last two schools, rejecting to a large degree the more pessimistic school of Freud with its emphasis on preordained behaviour.

Brock's research on the major influences behind coaching has led her to focus on those who shaped the coaching industry from many diverse disciplines, including sports and philosophy. But the two most dominant disciplines are psychology and business.

Psychologists who have influenced coaching

Alfred Adler

Born: 1879
Nationality: Austrian-American

Alfred Adler, Freud's erstwhile colleague, broke away from psychoanalysis to form his own independent school of psychotherapy and personality theory. He is also known for devising the concept of the "inferiority complex" as well as that of "feminism", of which he was strongly in favour. His main contribution to coaching is that he viewed individuals as always striving towards a goal, whereas Freud saw them as enslaved by their past. Essentially optimistic in outlook, he believed that people possessed the ability to devise their own solutions, which is the cornerstone of all coaching practice.

Chris Argyris

Born: 1923
Nationality: American

Chris Argyris, a psychologist, was one of the first to develop team-building sessions with senior executives and CEOs in the 1960s.

He focused much of his early research on exploring the impact of formal organisational structures, control systems and management on individuals. He later shifted his focus to organisational change, looking in particular at the behaviour of senior executives. His influence on coaching is seen as an indirect one in that he emphasised the discrepancy between what individuals say and what they do.

Richard Bandler

Born: 1950
Nationality: American

Richard Bandler, a psychotherapist, was a disciple of Fritz Perls (see page 18) and went on to co-found neuro-linguistic programming (NLP) with John Grinder, an associate professor of linguistics. NLP, a so-called science of the mind, has taken the world by storm over the past two decades. Bandler has been hailed as a genius by some but heavily criticised by others for inventing what they deem a "pseudoscience". In 2006 the American Specialty Health Organisation (ASH), which has over 13m members and provides fitness and well-being programmes to individuals and companies, said that it was not aware of any valid published studies proving the scientific plausibility, diagnostic utility, or clinical efficacy of NLP. Bandler has also been mired in controversy, not least for his acrimonious split with Grinder in the 1980s and his private life; in 1988 he was tried but acquitted of the murder of a prostitute.

Nevertheless, the techniques he and Grinder developed have allowed individuals to shed, sometimes in minutes, phobias and bad memories that have plagued them through life. Only by detaching your mind from such fears can they be shed, he asserts. Further therapeutic techniques flowed from his work with hypnotist Milton Erickson (see page 15). Neuro refers to the nervous system and the mental pathways of the five senses; linguistic refers to language and its usage; and programming is borrowed from computer science. These three elements were combined to create a therapeutic technology that could manipulate people's thoughts, emotions and deeds, which is why many people remain distrustful of NLP or of at least of its practice by those who are unprincipled.

People, according to Bandler, are motivated by either pleasure or an absence of pain, with the majority motivated by the latter. By repositioning people towards motivation and away from pain or fear, you could open up new possibilities in human endeavour. NLP has been widely embraced by some in the coaching industry, largely because of its emphasis on motivation, goal achievement, relationships, self-esteem and performance.

Robert Dilts

Born: 1955
Nationality: American

If the unorthodox Bandler was the wild man of NLP, then Robert Dilts, a disciple of both Bandler and Milton Erickson (see page 15), helped to make neuro-linguistic programming more acceptable to the mainstream. He is best known for his work on beliefs and values as well as for injecting an element of spirituality into the methodology. His sphere of influence has been predominantly in education, health and leadership. Some of his techniques and models include "re-imprinting". An imprint is a significant experience or period of life when belief or a series of beliefs took root and became core to an individual's identity. Re-imprinting is a device used to find the resources necessary to change such fundamental beliefs. Dilts also produced the *The Encyclopedia of Systemic NLP* with Judith DeLozier.

Mihaly Csikszentmihalyi

Born: 1934
Nationality: Hungarian-American

Mihaly Csikszentmihalyi (pronounced chick-sent-me-hi) belongs broadly to the same school of positive psychology as Seligman but has developed a slightly different perspective on happiness. In his book *Flow: the Psychology of Optimal Experience*, he argues that happiness pursued for its own sake is a mistake. Genuine happiness, in his view, comes from being powerful and true to ourselves through love of our chosen work or activity. In an interview with *Wired* magazine, Csikszentmihalyi, who is now at the Drucker

School of Management at Claremont Graduate University in California, defined flow as:

> *being completely involved in an activity for its own sake. The ego falls away. Time flies. Every action, movement, and thought follows inevitably from the previous one, like playing jazz. Your whole being is involved, and you're using your skills to the utmost.*

Formerly head of the Psychology Department at the University of Chicago, Csikszentmihalyi took those ideas and used them to discover what makes some individuals unusually creative in their ability to change the ways we do things or change how we view the world through their respective fields of endeavour. His book *Creativity: Flow and the Psychology of Discovery and Invention* is the culmination of some 30 years of research into the subject. It also includes interviews with over 90 people whom he identified as having an extraordinary impact on the modern world, including 14 Nobel Prize winners. Among them were Margaret Butler, a mathematician; Jonas Salk, a biologist; Ravi Shankar, a musician; and Benjamin Spock, a pediatrician and author. All of his interviewees were at least 60, which allowed Csikszentmihalyi sufficient opportunity to explore their mature talents. Among his conclusions were that:

▶ environment and timing are important to creativity – Michelangelo may not have been able to create his masterpieces had he been born 50 years earlier, before the rise of the great artistic patrons;

▶ creative breakthroughs are chiefly the result of years of hard work, rather than brilliant flukes;

▶ mastery of basic skills and knowledge of particular fields of endeavour are the precursor to creative flowering;

▶ exceptionally creative people are generally happy, rather than tortured geniuses;

▶ performance at school or college may not really matter – Einstein was considered a dunce by some of his teachers;

▶ losing a parent early on in life, preferably a father, is a great motivator – it also helps to have a loving but pushy mother;

▶ a poor or at least a suitably intellectual or Bohemian family background is more conducive to fostering exceptional talent than one of middle class affluence.

Csikszentmihalyi's work resonates strongly with coaching in its emphasis on self-reliance and fulfilment through self-improvement and high performance.

Albert Ellis

Born: 1913
Nationality: American

Albert Ellis is an important figure in the development of cognitive behavioural therapy (CBT), the way in which irrational thoughts can be replaced by rational ones. CBT runs counter to decades of earlier Freudian psychoanalysis, which asserts that we are ruled by repressed desires. Ellis, who was also one of the fathers of the "sexual revolution" of the 1960s, has found strong favour with contemporary coaches, particularly for his use of "talk therapy". If you experience terrible and frightening emotions you need to track back through the sequence of thoughts that gave rise to them in order to target and challenge the underlying and usually "irrational" assumption that fathered them. If we think something is going to be a catastrophe, it usually ends up as one. The key to the good life, asserted Ellis, is to apply rationality to the most irrational aspects of ourselves: our emotions.

Milton H. Erickson

Born: 1901
Nationality: American

Milton Erickson was the father of hypnotherapy – he brought it into the psychology mainstream, where others such as Freud more than four decades before him had tried and failed. He is perhaps most famous for his emphasis on the unconscious mind as something both creative and problem solving. "It is really amazing what people can do," said the former asylum doctor. "Only they don't know what they can do." His work, a precursor to neuro-linguistic programming (see Richard Bandler, page 12) focused on asking rather than telling and solution-focused therapy. The other thing that Erickson was noted for, which also resonates strongly with coaching, was his expertise in building rapport with his patients. Rapport was far more important to him than background history. When addressing behavioural problems, he would imitate what his patients were telling him, or doing, in order to help them see how irrational and ridiculous they were being. For example, he mirrored the actions of a beautiful but wilful 12-year-old female patient, who would fly into rages and start wrecking rooms and kicking strangers. He started copying her actions in a local hospital, tearing plaster from the walls and even ripping the clothes off a passing nurse, leaving her underwear exposed, at which point the profoundly shocked girl remonstrated with him and from then on saw the folly of her own extreme behaviour and was reportedly cured.

Daniel Goleman

Born: 1946
Nationality: America

With a doctorate in psychology from Harvard, Daniel Goleman combined his academic background with strong journalistic talent. But it was only after alighting on the papers of two obscure academics, John Mayer and Peter Salovey, linking emotions to intelligence, that Goleman, a *New York Times* columnist, went on to make it big with his bestselling book *Emotional Intelligence*. The book, which appealed to the general reader as well as the business world, was centred on the belief that emotional intelligence, or EQ as it has become known – the possession of abilities such as resilience, initiative, optimism, adaptability to change and empathy towards others – is what really makes certain individuals excel at work and in life. Goleman went on to explain why such skills, sometimes described as character, personality, maturity or "soft skills", matter more to modern employers, who no longer compete just on products but also on how well they deploy their people. His research, conducted at 120 companies, revealed that two-thirds of the personal attributes attributed to excellence at work could be accurately described as emotional competencies, skills that went beyond normal intelligence.

In his later work, he went on to describe what he regarded as the five core emotional competencies: self-awareness; self-regulation – the ability to be conscientious and delay gratification to achieve our goals, the awareness of our own strengths and shortcomings; motivation; empathy – the ability to tune into others' feelings and thinking; and social skills. Goleman's work resonates strongly with coaches such as Marshall Goldsmith (see page 90) in its assertion that senior executives fail when "they rise to the level of their own incompetence", and go no further. It is their failings in the key competencies that hold them back, asserts Goleman: they are too rigid, too arrogant in their dealings with others or too unwilling to change.

Carl Jung

Born: 1875
Nationality: Swiss

Carl Jung, the founder of analytical psychology, emphasised understanding of the psyche through exploration of dreams, art, world religion, mythology and philosophy – something that had previously been ignored and rejected by the science of psychology. For Jung, the outer world, which primitive man went to such lengths to document, provided the means to understanding the inner self. He believed that the goal in life was "individuation" of self, the coming together of two opposites – the conscious and unconscious mind – so that a person's potential could be fulfilled. He also emphasised spiritual awakening during the second half of life – a basic need, he argued, that psychology, for all its modernity and sophistication, had failed to address. His methodology also involved patients undertaking life reviews as part of his efforts to explore human consciousness, a practice widely emulated in coaching today.

Abraham Maslow

Born: 1908
Nationality: American

Abraham Maslow, the son of uneducated Russian-Jewish immigrants, was a student of Adler and the father of humanistic and transpersonal psychology. Instead of focusing on ill or disturbed people, which had been the natural domain of most forms of psychology, Maslow came up with the theory of "self-actualisation". Although another psychologist, Kurt Goldstein, introduced the term, it was Maslow who really developed the concept. It describes those rare and often unconventional individuals who are both moral and highly effective in all that they do and who possess the potential to transform society for the better. Maslow's theory has strong echoes of Aristotle, the Athenian philosopher who wrote: "In the area of human life the honours and rewards fall to those who show their good qualities." His theory also resonates with coaches such as Gallwey and Whitmore because of its emphasis on developing individual potential and nobility of purpose. However, some psychologists dismiss it as utopian nonsense.

Fritz Perls

Born: 1893
Nationality: German-American

Fritz Perls, who grew up in Bohemian Berlin in the 1930s, was one of the co-founders of Gestalt therapy, an experiential psychotherapy that deals with an individual's experience in the present moment. A refugee from Hitler's Germany, Perls arrived in 1964 at the Esalen Institute in California, the engine-room of change, which generated many of the more outlandish ideas behind America's social revolution of the 1960s. Perls's big belief was that modern men and women spent too much time thinking and not enough time experiencing, feeling and doing. His slogan "lose your mind and come to your senses" appealed strongly to prevailing hippy sentiment. So too did Perls's rejection of traditional psychology's tendency to interpret and judge. Too much analysis made people neurotic, he asserted. His "empty chair technique", aimed at heightening awareness, has been widely emulated by sections of the coaching community. It involves asking people to explain and monitor what they are doing at a precise moment. Only by being totally in the present, argued Perls, could you leave abstract worries behind. Those who complained of boredom and impatience with such experiments were usually dismissed as neurotic or at least "lacking in actuality".

Carl Rogers

Born: 1902
Nationality: American

Carl Rogers, like Albert Ellis (see page 15) and other humanist psychologists, emphasised the importance of the client-therapist relationship over technique. A good relationship would help clients find within themselves the capacity for growth and personal development. He radically shifted the emphasis in psychology from the problematic to the possible and a rejection of the psychologist as the superior player in such relationships. His emphasis was on the client's goals, with the client leading much of the process, rather than the more traditional emphasis on "fixing them". He believed that only clients could heal themselves. Like coaching his approach was all about acceptance and support in a non-judgmental environment and above all it emphasised the importance of listening.

Martin Seligman

Born: 1942
Nationality: American

For a man so immersed in positive psychology, Martin Seligman is no ray of sunshine. The self-confessed "grouch" spent much of his earlier life as a conventional clinical psychologist, trying to help people with mental illnesses or neuroses get better. "I wasn't good at it, I liked the sound of my own voice too much," he confesses. He also recalls attempting to cure a woman he was treating of her depression. "I was convinced that if I could cure her, I would make her happy." But when her depression was finally cured, he discovered there was no well-being, only an empty person. It was not until some years later when his daughter, then a small child, berated her father for his irascibility that he underwent a profound personal and professional conversion. "I had spent 50 years enduring mostly wet weather in my soul ... I resolved to change." His psychology bestseller, *Authentic Happiness: Using the*

New Positive Psychology to Realize Your Potential for Lasting Fulfilment, has been described as a manifesto for a new type of psychology where the emphasis is all on learned optimism, rather than on "fixing" depression and anxiety, no matter how laudable that endeavour. Much of his research at the University of Philadelphia focused on the causes of happiness as well as exposing some of its fallacies. Grandma was right, money does not bring lasting happiness (but then again neither does grinding poverty): purchasing power has increased dramatically in countries such as the United States and Japan, yet life satisfaction has remained unchanged for the past half century, while the similarly affluent Swiss are among the happiest in the world. In the UK, life satisfaction has actually decreased, for children at least, with the UK coming bottom for child well-being in a league table of 21 industrialised countries, according to a 2007 UNICEF report. Marriage, religious belief and sociability increase happiness, while individualism, with its sometimes unrealistic belief that every conceivable success is open to us, as well as the erosion of nationhood can lead to depression. His work resonates with coaching in its emphasis on strengths rather than on weaknesses.

Ken Wilber

Born: 1949
Nationality: American

Ken Wilber, a writer on philosophy and a former medical student, invented integral theory, an approach which he claims is truly cross-cultural, inclusive and comprehensive and one that can be applied to virtually all disciplines, such as law, business, medicine, spirituality, education and coaching. He began developing his theory while still in medical school at Duke University, where he grew increasingly disenchanted by what he came to regard as the narrowness of conventional scientific teaching and practice. Instead he found himself obsessed by the great three universal questions: what is the meaning of life; why am I here; and what is the morally good life? In his first book, *The Spectrum of Consciousness,* he set out on what would become a lifelong odyssey to find out the answers. His writing combines eastern and western spirituality, psychology, biology, cultural theory and other strands of contemporary thinking to create what the author calls "integral psychology". Wilber attempts to bridge science and religion and explain the dynamics of human consciousness and moral development, as well as to speculate on the future evolution of mankind. He lives in Boulder, Colorado, where he has established the Integral Institute, described as "a spiritual United Nations". His admirers include former American president Bill Clinton, who quoted the philosopher at the World Economic Forum in Davos in 2007:

> You know, the problem is, the world needs to be more integrated but it requires a level of consciousness that's way up here, an ability to see beyond the differences among us.

Gurus who have influenced coaching

Ken Blanchard

Born: 1939
Nationality: American

Ken Blanchard is best known as the co-author of *The One Minute Manager*, a book that he wrote in 1981 with children's writer Spencer Johnson. A heavyweight business academic, Blanchard discovered a talent for making the clever and complex clever and simple. "I always write as I talk," he says. *The One Minute Manager* has sold more than 13m copies and is a distillation of Blanchard's brand of no-nonsense leadership philosophy, a theme he has elaborated in more than 40 books, mostly written in collaboration with others. He set up The Ken Blanchard Companies, an international management training and consulting firm in San Diego, in 1979 with his wife Margie. Much of the organisation's work was based on the situational leadership model that he initially devised with a fellow academic, Paul Hersey, in 1969 and later simplified in the One Minute Manager series. Situational leadership outlines four different leadership styles that can be adopted depending on the situation or task involved. These are:

▶ directing – where the leader tells and shows the follower or employee what needs to be done;

▶ coaching – where there is two-way communication and where the leader directs but also seeks ideas and suggestions from subordinates;

▶ supporting – where the leader focuses on motivation and confidence issues but leaves the decisions and task to the employee;

▶ delegating – where the leader provides high-level direction only, but leaves decision-making to the subordinate.

The effective leader, Blanchard says, will be able to move between the various styles of leadership, recognising that a follower will have different development levels for the different tasks required. Blanchard's company formed its own coaching arm in 2001 to support its leadership training programmes. Says Blanchard:

> *The goal of coaching is self-directed action. Coaches are not there to make people dependent on them, but to make people help themselves.*

Much of Blanchard's later work reflects his spiritual beliefs:

> *Too many leaders act as if the sheep ... their people ... are there for the benefit of the shepherd, not that the shepherd has responsibility for the sheep.*

Peter Block

Born: 1939
Nationality: American

For a management consultant Peter Block is remarkably fiery. The author of the much praised guide to his industry, *Flawless Consulting: A Guide to Getting Your Expertise Used*, first published in 1980, is not just disillusioned with much of American big business but positively exploding with bile and spleen over what he regards as its economic and moral failures. He fulminates:

> *We're talking about the end of competition where power is so concentrated among the large corporations we have lost all sense of market reality.*

Globalisation, he argues, is not so much about freewheeling entre-preneurialism, of which he is broadly in favour, but a cynical exer-cise in unfettered consumerism, of which he is not. He compares some of his colleagues in management consultancy to Davy Crock-ett, a 19th-century American frontiersman who died in the Battle of the Alamo. Crockett's reputation has recently taken a nosedive after being attacked by revisionist historians such as Jeff Long, who dismisses him as "an ageing, semi-literate squatter of average talent". Consultants are undergoing a similar reputational down-grade. They are the shock troops of this process, Block argues, hired by the big corporations, many of which have little interest in free and open competition, to gain a toehold for consumerism and by so doing set about destroying local cultures and communities.

Like many of the elder statesmen still inhabiting the corporate plains, Block, now in his 70s, believes there must be a return to a less self-serving business ethic. In his later work, *Stewardship: Choosing Service Over Self-Interest*, he argues that the organisations that succeed will be the ones that choose service and stewardship over self-interest. They will hold themselves accountable to those over whom they exercise power. Such an exercise, he says, calls for a new way of thinking. The result will be to replace a system built on self-interest, dependency and control with one based on service, responsibility and partnership. Block's quirky combination of hard-nosed consultancy expertise, a revolutionary embrace of values and a call to arms has made him something of a popular folk hero in certain coaching circles. On a practical level coaches have learned much from the practical intervention techniques out-lined in his books. A coach, like a consultant, is trying to gain influ-ence over a group or individual but has no direct power to make changes or implement programmes. However, some might baulk at Block's suggestion that in self-serving organisations, coaching has been downgraded to a badge of honour for anyone at middle manager grade and above. "It is a mechanism to enable them to cope with a harsh and largely dysfunctional system."

David Cooperrider

Born: 1954
Nationality: American

David Cooperrider is widely credited with devising the methodology of appreciative inquiry with its apparently simplistic assertion that organisations are not all about problems that need to be solved, but are created as solutions to a particular challenge or to satisfy a need of society at a given time. In short, Cooperrider, who is associate professor of organisational behaviour at Case Western University's Weatherhead School of Management, is to organisational development what Seligman is to positive psychology. Appreciative inquiry offers a positive, strengths-based approach to organisational development and change management. He asserts:

> *I have found that it does not help, in the long run, to begin my inquiries from the standpoint of the world as a problem to be solved. I am more effective, quite simply, as long as I can retain the spirit of inquiry of the everlasting beginner.*

Cooperrider, whose work has found strong favour with coaches, based his appreciative inquiry on the assumption that individuals respond more favourably to positive affirmations of their talents and qualities than to criticism about perceived inadequacies. Adopting this technique, coaches might praise and affirm the qualities of the people they are coaching and gently challenge them, rather than directly confronting them, to find their own solutions to the issues or problems under discussion. Cooperrider's work has also found favour in the wider world. His appreciative inquiry technique has been deployed at a series of dialogues held by the world's top 25 religious leaders, following the establishment of the United Religions Initiative by the Dalai Lama, who said:

> *If only the world's religious leaders could just know each other, the world will be a better place.*

Stephen Covey

Born: 1932
Nationality: American

> *Management is efficiency in climbing the ladder of success;
> leadership determines whether the ladder is leaning against
> the right wall.*

Harvard-educated Stephen Covey, who wrote *The Seven Habits of
Highly Effective People*, from which the above quotation is taken, is
a Mormon from Salt Lake City. He served out his Mormon mission
in the UK, before returning to academia where he became a professor of organisational behaviour at Brigham Young University. But
Covey, a gifted preacher, was destined to reach a much wider audience than just his fellow Mormons. The self-help mogul, whose
best-selling book has sold more than 15m copies, distilled down
his principles for management success into seven bite-sized pearls
of wisdom that appeal not only to aspiring corporate leaders, but
also to a wider audience that includes housewives and troubled
teenagers. He also invented a two-by-two matrix for effective time
management. It was designed to help prioritise activities into either
the important or the urgent. Thus activities could be urgent and
important; important but not urgent; urgent but not important; and
neither urgent nor important. Effective people, says Covey, concentrate on the second of those categories: the important but not
urgent. That way they avoid the need for constant crisis management of the urgent and important.

Covey makes no proprietary claims on his seven principles or
habits. He studied several books about personal success for his
doctoral dissertation, including Dale Carnegie's *How to Win Friends
and Influence People*, before writing his own book. The seven
habits, he says, are based on universal truths found in all the major
world religions and are largely a matter of common sense, though
less easy to put into practice. In the 1980s, when he first came to
wider prominence, Covey emphasised the importance of meaning,
or essential goodness, in a corporate world that had hitherto been
dominated by time management and theories of efficiency. Covey
may not have regarded himself as a coach, but much of his work
can be viewed as a template for self-coaching.

The seven principles are as follows:

▶ Be proactive – don't let the past hold you captive.

▶ Begin with the end in mind – work out the ultimate objective and work back.

▶ Put first things first.

▶ Think win-win – victory should not be at everyone else's expense.

▶ Seek first to understand, then to be understood – without empathy there is no influence.

▶ Synergise – which comes from the exercise of all the other habits to bring about additional benefits that could not be predicted.

▶ Sharpen the saw – taken from the metaphor of the woodcutter who does not stop to sharpen his saw because he's too busy chopping down a tree.

Covey went on to establish the Covey Leadership Centre, which merged in 1997 with Franklin Quest to form FranklinCovey, a global firm specialising in management and leadership training. In his most recent work, *The Eighth Habit*, Covey returned to his spiritual roots. The eighth "habit" is about finding your authentic voice. Covey asserts that it is no longer enough to be merely effective in today's increasingly complex knowledge worker age. He says:

> *We enjoy greater autonomy yet at the same time we struggle to feel engaged, fulfilled and passionate.*

Peter Drucker

Born: 1909
Nationality: Austrian-American

> *In the next economic downturn there will be an outbreak of bitterness and contempt for those super-corporate chieftains who pay themselves millions.*
>
> Written in 1997

A prolific writer and business guru who died at the age of 95 in 2005, Peter Drucker is widely regarded as the "father of modern management". A man of great charm and modesty, he accurately predicted the major business developments of the late 20th century including:

▶ privatisation;

▶ the rise of Japan as an economic world power;

▶ the pre-eminence of marketing and brands;

▶ the emergence of the information society;

▶ the rise of the "knowledge worker" – a term which he coined and developed as far back as the 1970s, long before others realised how knowledge would supersede in importance raw materials, manual labour and increasingly even capital in the modern economy.

Drucker may have foreseen the rise of the modern corporation, but in old age he grew increasingly disenchanted with the way that corporations behaved. He was appalled at the level of pay awarded to *Fortune* 500 CEOS, which had exploded to several hundred times that of the average worker. As far back as 1984, he argued that CEO compensation should be no more than 20 times what the rank and file made, especially at corporations where thousands of workers were being laid off. "This is morally and socially unforgivable," Drucker wrote, "and we will pay a heavy price for it." Drucker never conformed to the image of the conventional management consultant. "My job", he once told a corporate client, "is to ask questions. It's your job to provide answers." It is small wonder then that so much of Drucker's work has had a profound influence on coaching. When asked by *Fortune* 500 CEO coach Marshall Goldsmith about his own personal mission, Drucker responded: "My mission is to help other people achieve their goals – assuming they are not immoral or unethical."

Werner Erhard

Born: 1935
Nationality: American

Known as John Paul Rosenberg before reinventing his name and life, Werner Erhard is widely regarded as the man who gave the human development movement its popular appeal and one of the most significant influences behind coaching. Once described by *Newsweek* as "a celebrity guru who retails enlightenment", the former car salesman remains a highly controversial figure, not least for his sometimes authoritarian and reportedly unorthodox training methods that sometimes resulted in tears and trainees being prevented from taking comfort breaks, all deployed in the name of personal transformation. Erhard, who was originally from Philadelphia, was apparently inspired by the self-help literature of Napoleon Hill, author of *Think and Grow Rich*, published in 1937, as well as by Scientology and the personal development training run by Texas-based Mind Dynamics. He headed out to California where in 1971 he established EST – which means "it is" in Latin but also stands for Erhard Seminars Training – his own large group awareness training company through which he grew rich selling personal transformation programmes.

Coaches frequently cite the largely self-taught Erhard, whose teachings were based on a mishmash of theories and beliefs from the works of Freud, Maslow, Gestalt, Heidegger, Zen Buddhism and Dale Carnegie, as the person who has exerted the most profound influence on their work. The late Thomas Leonard (see page 81), founder of Coach U, the International Coach Federation, Coachville and the International Association of Coaches, was an EST employee in the late 1980s.

Although Erhard, whose style could be highly directional, was not regarded as a coach, he introduced many of coaching's later concepts to large numbers of people, especially his ideas about self-responsibility. It is estimated that more than 700,000 people attended his courses during his ten years in the business. He also brought his personal development ideas to business from 1984 through his consultancy, Transformational Technologies. By this stage, Erhard had already teamed up with Fernando Flores, a former Chilean senator and businessman, and their courses ran under the banner of the Forum. After Erhard announced his departure from the company in 1984 EST was dissolved, and in 1991 he left the United States for Mexico. He sold his training companies' intellectual property rights to former employees, who set up Landmark Education. The company now operates in 50 offices in 24 countries, with reported annual revenues of $90m in 2007, and continues to expand and develop Erhard's original ideas.

Tom Peters

Born: 1942
Nationality: American

Tom Peters, a former naval officer, wrote *In Search of Excellence* with fellow McKinsey management consultant Robert Waterman in 1982. The book, based on the simple idea that if you engender decision-making at all levels of a company you can effectively solve problems without the need for costly additional business processes, became a national bestseller. "Leaders don't create followers, they create more leaders," he said.

The phenomenal success of the book was reinforced by Peters's innate showmanship. He hosted a follow-up TV series based on the book on America's Public Broadcasting Service. Unlike the shy and retiring Waterman, who remained at McKinsey for many years, Peters quickly departed from the firm to set up on his own as a motivational guru in the global business arena, where he repeatedly demonstrated his unique talent for working a crowd of normally staid business types to near-idolatrous worship of his own particular brand of American business wisdom. Kathryn Harrigan, professor of business leadership at Columbia Business School, attributed Peters's success to the fact that Americans are into cults and particularly the cult of personality:

> They are all looking for the recipe of success and Tom Peters made the best job of that. People know exactly where to place him.

In his later work, the ever-populist Peters became preoccupied with change in a chaotic world. He also began to focus on self-improvement, something that resonates strongly with coaching. Instead of his earlier message to corporate America to start pushing power down to its winning teams, he exhorted workers to break out of their cubicles and start taking control of their lives by polishing up their résumés, to think of themselves as a brand and to regard their corporations as mere stepping stones.

Peter Senge

Born: 1947
Nationality: American

Peter Senge studied aerospace engineering at Stanford University before completing his master's degree on social systems modelling at MIT's Sloan School of Management. A quiet unassuming man, a firm advocate of meditation and an expert in organisational behaviour, Senge was named in 1999 by the *Journal of Business Strategy* as one of the 24 men and women considered to have the greatest impact on the way business is conducted. He might have remained in relative academic obscurity had it not been for the success of his book, *The Fifth Discipline: The Art and Practice of The Learning Organisation*, in which he set out his beliefs on organisational learning. His big idea was that successful and enduring organisations required continuous learning if they were to secure long-term viability. He describes what he regarded as the five essential elements or disciplines of successful organisations:

1 Personal mastery – involves vision, an objective assessment of underlying reality and the motivation to pursue the goals we truly desire through continuous learning and self-improvement.

2 Mental models – to develop an awareness of the way in which individuals and organisations think, and to constantly challenge underlying assumptions.

3 Shared vision – to create models or images of the future that all individuals within an organisation can accept and embrace.

4 Team learning – using group dialogue and discussion to help the team become more effective than individual members would be on their own.

5 The ability to see the organisation as a whole, with its own thinking and behaviour patterns separate from the individuals who make up the various constituent parts.

Senge says:

We often spend so much time coping with problems along our path that we forget why we are on that path in the first place. The result is that we only have a dim, or even inaccurate, view of what's really important to us.

Some of Senge's ideas have been dismissed as utopian or overly "idealistic" in some quarters, but his focus on change and learning has provided a strong foundation for group coaching and even individual coaching with its emphasis on using leadership in organisations to enhance the potential of individuals to work towards common goals.

Edgar Schein

Born: 1928
Nationality: Hungarian-American

Edgar Schein, a professor at MIT Sloan School of Management, is credited with inventing the term "corporate culture". He began his career as a social psychologist and quickly went on to make his mark through his groundbreaking research on indoctrination. As a former US army captain, he interviewed American POWs returning home from the Korean war and discovered how the breakdown of group identity could encourage individuals to inform on friends, make false confessions and generally commit high treason without any need for physical coercion. But it was his interview technique that made Schein, a pupil of psychologist Carl Rogers (see page 19), so successful at gathering such candid material:

If one is trying to elicit information in an area that may be socially or emotionally sensitive, do not ask about it. Instead rely on a chronology, on a natural history of events and let the sensitive stuff come out in its own way ... in other words I encouraged them to tell their story in their own way.

This experience went on to inform much of his work in the corporate arena in the 1950s when large organisations, such as General Electric, saw no irony in possessing a "GE Indoctrination Centre". Schein, who also studied the methods used by the Spanish Inquisition, says:

What was particularly exciting at that time was the discovery that different methods of indoctrination throughout history bore incredible similarity to each other.

The other area in which Schein became involved and which he wrote about in *Career Dynamics* (1978) was the way in which organisations constrained individuals, partly because of misconceptions by those organisations of what people really wanted. Yet again it was his technique in soliciting such information that linked his work so strongly to coaching. In 1969 he wrote *Process Consultation*, which established the link between what Schein called "low key inquiry" and its ability to help clients resolve their own problems. The process consultation methods that Schein wrote about contained many of the characteristics of coaching. However, many companies currently deploying coaching might not feel entirely comfortable with his apparent preference for a non-directive approach. Schein distinguishes between two types of coaching: one in which the client defines the help he or she requires; and another in which a manager brings in a coach to help an individual improve job performance or overcome perceived deficiencies. He says:

If an organisation "imposes" a coach and a predetermined direction of learning then by definition we are dealing with indoctrination, not coaching.

Mentoring: the world we have lost

> The prince replied, wise in his own way too, "How can I greet him Mentor, even approach the king? I'm hardly adept at subtle conversation. Someone my age might feel shy, what's more, interrogating an older man."
>
> Odyssey, 2.300–304

The accelerating complexity of life has put paid to more traditional notions of mentoring, but can modern reconstructs prove as effective?

If we think hard enough, we can usually come up with someone who has had an enormous influence on our lives. It could be a favourite uncle or grandmother, or a teacher or someone who has used his or her influence and position to help smooth your career and never asks for anything in return. In short, an ideal mentor in the traditional mould has a profound respect for youth, sees potential in individuals that they or others cannot recognise, and is a wise but economical counsellor, a prodigious listener and a friend.

Mentors are still around us, but we often have trouble recognising them. The image of the wise grey-head is no longer a positive stereotype in western culture, particularly in Anglo-Saxon-based ones, where old age has become less associated with wisdom and experience and more with decline and decay.

A.A. Gill, a British writer and newspaper columnist, depicted the average Briton's attitude to the elderly in an article in the *Sunday Times* in March 2009:

The great terror of our age is age. We would rather consign the old to a netherworld, a waiting room where they are out of mind and out of sight. The fear is plainly not of the old: it is that we will become them. The old are the zombies at the end of our own home horror movies.

Yet the wisdom and experience of the old are often worth listening to, especially during times of great change. Those that forget the lessons of history are doomed to repeat them.

Richard Russell, an American financial pundit now aged 84, has been writing his *Dow Theory Letters* for 50 years and has an ardent following among investors. He was four years old when the Great Crash happened and remembers some of the hardships he encountered growing up in the 1930s. In one of his recent letters he says:

People in this country [America] don't realise how bad things can be. I lived through the Great Depression. I remember people standing in bread lines. It was hard to get a job, any job, back then. But now, you see the restaurants are still full. People are still spending money. They may be worried and they may be beginning to save, but there's no sense of urgency. And there's a rally on Wall Street. You know, every bear market produces a rally. You can expect the market to retrace its steps by one- to two-thirds.

Russell may prove not to have been right, but his perspective is forged by his own experiences of the Great Depression.

The chances are that if you mention the word "mentor" today outside the UK or the United States, you will draw blank looks from the faces around you. In France, for example, where historical mentoring precedents abound, people will recognise *"le coaching"* but not mentoring in the traditional sense of the word. You will also struggle to find much in the way of literature on the subject. Mentoring does not necessarily mean the same thing in the UK as it does in the United States.

In this book mentors are people who:

▶ give advice and make expert recommendations;

▶ bring personal experience to bear;

▶ open doors and use their contacts and networks to help the people who are being mentored;

▶ are usually, but not always, unpaid.

Like coaches the best mentors also:

▶ ask insightful questions;

▶ listen carefully;

▶ are empathetic;

▶ are generous of spirit and time.

▶ help engender self-awareness.

Really good mentors are rare, says Anne Scoular, managing director of a London-based coaching firm, Meyler Campbell, and a member of the Worldwide Association of Business Coaches (WABC) Expert Review Panel:

> It's quite simple. Mentoring and traditional "teaching-style" coaching put in advice, guidance, information, suggestions, contacts, etc – while non-directive coaching pulls out the capacities people have within. In practice, good mentors can coach as well as mentor. Good coaches will, unquestionably, put in some information, tools or data, when they believe it is in the best interests of the client, but judiciously.

Scoular believes mentoring is easy for people, "since our societies encourage telling", while coaching "takes time and effort to learn". She suggests that those learning coaching skills need to "unlearn telling, to hold back and draw the answer from the client".

Mentor's origins

The original Mentor sprang from the Trojan wars, a period of history largely lost in the mists of time and legend, but which is believed by historians to have occurred around 1190BC. Although that event may not appear to have much relevance in the 21st century, the same uncertainty, fear and sweeping technological change affected people then as they do now. The Trojan wars coincided with a period when Mycenaean civilisation – the age of the

Greeks – was giving way to that of the Dorians, who were to supplant Greek bronze with swords of harder metal.

The *Iliad* was penned some 400 years later, towards the end of the Greek Dark Ages, when Homer and others were urging the aristocracy to bring democracy to the emerging political councils, or *polis*. Much of the *Iliad* can be seen as an argument against individual acts of valour and heroism, the glorification of the warrior code, which ultimately proved so ruinous to Greek and Trojan alike. Today there is similar change, but the speed with which it is happening would have been unimaginable to the Greeks, even the wily Odysseus, whose long journey to the wars and back on a series of particularly slow boats took him away for 20 years or so.

Can Mentor cope with complexity?

There is a strangely disturbing cult video on YouTube, made by blogger Karl Fisch. It consists of a series of stark graphics showing just how swiftly the information age and its underpinning technology are changing tomorrow's world, today. Against the backdrop of DJ Fatboy Slim's robotic dance rhythm *Right Here, Right Now*, the viewer is presented with a series of public pronouncements from a variety of official sources:

▶ today's learner will have 10–14 different jobs by the age of 38;

▶ the top ten in-demand jobs in 2010 did not exist in 2004;

▶ to reach an audience of 50m took radio 38 years, television 13 years, the internet four years and the iPod just two;

▶ a week's worth of news in the *New York Times* contains more information than someone living in the 18th century was likely to encounter in their entire life;

▶ by 2013 a $1,000 computer will exceed the computational capabilities of the entire human race; and

▶ in the six-minute, seven-second time span of the video, 67 babies will have been born in the United States, 274 in China and 395 in India.

Such stark statistics about the growing complexity of life have made many of us seek help. GE boss Jeff Imelt on a visit to his alma mater, Harvard Business School, in 2002 urged students to seek out the wisdom of mentors, "people you trust", to provide feedback and advice. It is hardly surprising that Mentor is enjoying a comeback. But can he – or she – cope with it all?

Not really, say Kathy Kram and Monica Higgins, respectively professor of organisational behaviour at Boston University's School of Management and associate professor at Harvard University's Graduate School of Education. In an article in the *Wall Street Journal* in September 2008 they wrote:

> *How can one teacher know enough to help you keep up with rapidly changing technology, as well as navigate the challenges of globalisation, a multicultural work force and team-based decision-making? Even people who have served as mentors often need help staying abreast of all these changes.*

A better approach, they say, is to create and cultivate a developmental network, a small group of people to whom you can turn for regular mentoring support and who have a genuine interest in your learning and development. "Think of it as your personal board of directors," they urge.

The composition of the group depends on where you are in your career and what you are looking for. If you are just setting out, you could turn to your boss or assigned mentor for help. But you should also look further, seeking out peers to get feedback on areas where you need to improve, such as public speaking or working in teams, they advise.

This view is endorsed by William Fries, head of the Thornburg International Value Fund, one of America's top fund managers, with some $18 billion under investment. Fries, who runs a close-knit, highly collegiate team, based in Santa Fe, New Mexico, nevertheless strongly resists the urge to institute the type of mentoring relationships from which he benefited as a younger man. He says:

> *I benefited greatly from them, but I'm acutely aware that the world has moved on. Everything is much more complex in the financial markets now than it was when I started out. To rely on the advice of just one mentor would be unwise.*

Times of great change demand dramatic reinvention and the rapid acquisition of new skills: a scribe may have to learn to wield a sword, or a shopkeeper to build defensive ditches. Similarly, when technology enables the transfer of capital, goods and services to whatever part of the globe where labour is cheapest, then many of the old certainties of life in the West, with its 60 years of virtually unbroken prosperity and welfare, may require similar levels of Darwinian adaptability and resourcefulness.

The Ancients knew this, but then the original mentor represented the perfect ideal. "He" was more often than not a "she" in the form of Athena, Goddess of Wisdom, in disguise, who came down from on high to guide Odysseus's son, Telemachus. Not everyone can rely on the same degree of immortal wisdom, or in having such a sensible young man to mentor as Telemachus.

Phoenix was also a mentor of sorts in the *Iliad*, but had rather less success. His protégé, Achilles, was headstrong and vainglorious. He struggled to teach Achilles how to be a speaker of words and a doer of deeds, but Achilles, though undoubtedly knowledgeable in the art of war, was not wise and ended up in disgrace, having subverted the original objectives of the war. Hence Homer's sarcastic vitriol (XVIII. 130–33):

> *But now to win glory*
> *And make some Trojan woman or deep-breasted*
> *Dardanian matron wipe the tears*
> *From her soft cheeks, make her sob and groan.*

Mentoring for social inclusion

Three thousand years on Mentor still lives, but he, or she, is more likely to be a socially conscious City worker imparting maths skills to the educationally disadvantaged, or a retired businessman who wants to give something back by helping a long-term prisoner set up an enterprise on release.

From the 1960s onwards the term "mentor" began to appear once more in Britain and America, but now as a specifically planned activity or intervention. Mentors no longer seek out their protégés informally, recognising some undefined quality that they wish to help develop, but are usually provided as part of a more formal mentoring network, which can typically be attached to a school, educational institution or work. There has been a spectacular expansion of mentoring in the United States, the UK and other countries over the past two decades, writes Helen Colley, an academic at Manchester Metropolitan University and author of *Mentoring for Social Inclusion*. It has become an integral aspect of initial education and professional development in business management, teaching and health care as well as many other fields.

It has also become a fashionable tool for policymakers, particularly as an intervention for improving the lot of disadvantaged young people. Mentoring for social inclusion has attracted numerous professionals and volunteers into such schemes. According to Colley, mentoring has gained almost "mythical status".

Youth mentoring, in particular, originated in the United States, and mentoring organisations have been in operation in one form or another for more than 100 years. For example, Big Brothers Big Sisters of America began by recruiting adult volunteers to help boys and girls who have been up before the courts. Such schemes involving mentors have generally been shown to lower instances of physical aggression and drug and substance abuse as well as induce better parent and peer relationships and higher educational attainment.

More recently, the US-based Mentor/National Mentoring Partnership was co-founded by Geoff Boisi, a former Goldman Sachs banker, and Ray Chambers, a philanthropist, in 1990 with the aim of providing every child in the United States who wants a mentor with one. The organisation has identified at least 17.6m young Americans who could benefit from mentoring, yet says only 3m are in formal, high-quality mentoring relationships.

Mentoring has also been a linchpin of the UK government's social inclusion initiatives. The UK has the highest incidence of absent father households in Europe and a low proportion of male primary-school teachers. As gun and knife crime soars, there has been increasing pressure to provide some form of positive male role model for children. There are 3,500 mentoring programmes currently running in the UK and in late 2008 Gordon Brown announced a £3.8m cash injection to help fund schemes in knife-crime hotspots.

The Chartered Institute of Personnel Development (CIPD) defines mentoring as:

> Developing a person's skills and knowledge so that their job performance improves, hopefully leading to the achievement of organisational objectives. It targets high performance and improvement at work, although it may also have an impact on an individual's private life. It usually lasts for a short period and focuses on specific skills and goals.

Unlike coaching, a mentoring relationship can last for a long time, or even in some cases a lifetime. Mentors and their protégés can remain in touch as friends long after the initial mentoring scheme has ended. It also tends to be more informal than any coaching relationship, which usually has a fixed time frame. Mentors impart their knowledge and experience, while coaches draw out the personal experiences and answers from the person being coached. In a mentoring relationship there is also likely to be a far greater emphasis on career and personal development, whereas the focus of coaching is usually on specific development areas.

Benefits to an organisation of mentoring are:

▶ better recruitment and retention – one study found that the loss of young graduates in the first expensive post-training year was cut by two-thirds;

▶ better succession planning;

▶ organisations become better at adapting to change;

▶ increased productivity through greater job satisfaction.

Benefits to the mentored person are:

▶ knowledge, technical and behavioural improvements;

▶ better planning of career goals;

▶ a wider network of influential contacts;

▶ increased confidence and self awareness;

▶ mentors also derive satisfaction from developing their colleagues and from passing on knowledge, skills and expertise.

The power of mentors

Some of the problems that beset earlier, more traditional models of mentoring still remain, predominantly dependency and even corruption. In business, for example, mentoring usually occurred when a senior person wished to pass on his wisdom and acquired knowledge to a selected protégé or favourite. Used wisely such relationships can be invaluable and powerful, but all too often they lead to charges of favouritism and overdependence.

Most famous historical pairings of this nature simply faded away, or outlived their usefulness and even damaged the person the relationship was most meant to serve. It could be argued that the wily fox Cardinal Richelieu indirectly helped sow the seeds of the French Revolution by investing so much power in the central figure of the king. Both he and his protégé, the slippery Cardinal Mazarin, moulded Louis XIII and Louis XIV respectively, but later successors of the "Sun King" possessed neither his brains nor his sense of realpolitik and as a result exposed the fatal weakness at the core of absolute monarchy – that it would crumble if the possessor of the office was not up to the job.

Nowadays there is no need to drink hemlock should the relationship sour. Latter day kings and heads of state continue to seek out mentors, an instinct that extends to all races and cultures, to help them with the demands of the role. It is often a parent or relative who initially assumes the mentoring role. It is said that John F. Kennedy's father, Joe, was his most important mentor. It was also his father who persuaded him to drop his plans to become a journalist in favour of politics. Yet Kennedy broke with his father over the latter's isolationism, a position that ruined Joe Kennedy's own political ambitions. He also ignored his father's more sensible advice not to run for the US vice-presidential nomination in 1956, a move that ended ignominiously for the young senator.

If anything, mentors are even more important to powerful women. Elizabeth I relied upon her wise counsellor, William Cecil, to help guide her through the treacherous early years of her reign. The young Queen Victoria similarly relied on Lord Melbourne, her prime minister.

It seems that many successful women have a powerful male influence early on in their childhoods, which could be a father or an uncle, says Sally Clarke, a London-based professional mentor. Margaret Thatcher, a former British prime minister, is a classic example in the extent to which she was influenced in political consciousness by her father, Alderman Alfred Roberts.

But it was her mentors later in life who arguably exerted a far greater influence on her and her political consciousness. Lady Thatcher might have remained a conventional politician had it not been for her later political mentors, who began to alter her views from 1974 onwards when she began her bid for the leadership of the Conservative Party, says Anthony Seldon, a political biographer and headmaster of Wellington College. There would have been no Thatcher revolution had it not been for men such as Keith Joseph, William Whitelaw, John Hoskyns and Airey Neave, who, says Seldon, "changed her very profoundly. They turned her into a radical".

Tony Blair, by contrast, does not appear to have been influenced by mentoring, either as a protégé or as a mentor to others, says Seldon, which is strange since his book, *Blair Unbound*, recounts the 20 events and 20 people who helped shape him:

> *Mandelson and Alastair Campbell were hugely influential during his first term, but I hesitate to call them mentors in the true sense of the word because they didn't believe in anything and in fact created a whole lot of trouble for him.*

It has been widely reported that the late Roy Jenkins, a former Labour politician who went on to found the Social Democratic Party, was a mentor in his later life to Blair, but again this assumption is challenged by Seldon:

> *I think that's rubbish. It suited Jenkins's vanity to think that and*

> *it suited Blair to let him imagine that. But all the things that Jenkins believed in politically – PR, Europe, and realignment of the left – were only being played at by Blair: he didn't really believe in them.*

True to the spirit of the age, as well as his more inclusive style of politics, Barack Obama's mentor is a woman, Valerie Jarrett, a well-heeled real-estate executive from Chicago, who took both him and his wife, Michelle, under her wing 20 years ago. She introduced them to a wealthier and better-connected Chicago than their own more modest backgrounds would have allowed, and which according to close political watchers was crucial to securing the money and contacts that were vital to Obama's "long-shot" Senate victory.

Jarrett, unlike some mentors, has not been overlooked by her appreciative protégés, who have taken her with them to the White House, where she will serve as a trusted senior adviser to President Obama – one of a handful of people who will be with him when key decisions are made. Like a proper mentor in the old-fashioned mould, she is described by Michelle Obama as someone who is "never afraid to tell you the truth", as well as a person she trusts implicitly. The president has also acknowledged her as an important sounding board for some of his most important decisions.

From a well-established black family of senior medics living in Chicago's wealthy Hyde Park area, Jarrett herself was a protégée of Chicago's mayor, Richard Daley, for whom she served as planning commissioner. She also acts as a mentor to other young people whose résumés she apparently keeps on file in case a prospective employer should call.

Attitudes to mentoring

Mentoring and power can make volatile bedfellows. A powerfully placed mentor can expedite a protégé's progress but also presents hidden dangers. If, for example, protégés attach themselves too closely to the coat-tails of mentors who subsequently fall from power, the protégés can suffer too.

This is one of the reasons modern politics, particularly in Anglo-Saxon cultures, pays lip service to mentoring's obvious benefits, particularly in the largely unpaid voluntary sector, but shies away from this more traditional form of patronage. This is not always a good thing, according to David Clutterbuck, one of the world's foremost authorities on mentoring:

> The modern political scene doesn't lend itself to a proper developmental model of mentoring. There is resistance to having thinking challenged in this way. What [modern politicians] care far more about is media reaction. It is all very shallow.

Indeed, it is worse than that, argues Vince Hagedorn, a former school teacher and IT entrepreneur who for several years ran a regional mentoring network, MENTFOR, a not-for-profit mentoring organisation covering the east of England. Loose thinking and lack of depth in our relationships have resulted in the government throwing away some of the obvious benefits that good mentoring relationships can bring:

> There was a time not so long ago when the UK government was quite receptive to the idea of mentoring but as soon as the coaches got wind of this they moved into Whitehall in a very big way and displaced us.

Significantly mentoring, with relatively few exceptions, is unpaid and voluntary, which in modern consumerist societies may mean – in contrast to the earlier mutuality practised by medieval trade guilds and the more philanthropic early Victorian capitalists – that it is neither valued nor appreciated.

This is because in the UK, in particular, government policy has been inconsistent and confused, says Hagedorn. MENTFOR involved giving small grants to both local businesses and the community in various mentoring projects, all of which, he says, were carefully monitored by independent assessors. In his own case, central government funding siphoned through the local development agency was pulled suddenly and without explanation after four years. It meant the end of several important community projects, one aimed at helping prisoners' children, along with the accumulated mentoring expertise and knowledge pool that had been built up over a four-year period.

UK government policy towards mentoring is at best confused, he says. This is largely because high-level policy initiatives by ministers have to permeate several layers of government, including the civil service, before they reach the people they are designed to help. Moreover, ministers are often replaced, or lose interest in initiatives; this also applies to government-funded quangos – the quasi-autonomous agencies set up to deliver such policies. There is little in the way of continuity. Survival of organisations such as MENTFOR will increasingly depend on more enduring methods of private funding at the grassroots level, says Hagedorn.

In earlier times mentoring may have been about power, but it was also about intimate personal relationships between craftsman and master or a ship's captain and his midshipman. Marrying the master's daughter was an accepted route to career advancement long before Charles Dickens began to write about it, and is still a popular option in Nigeria and other parts of Africa where traditional mentoring continues to flourish.

Peter Bamkole, who runs the Centre for Enterprise Development Services at the Pan-African University of Nigeria, explains how mentoring works:

> Basically you hire yourself out to your mentor and often you pay him – it's usually a him – for his support and patronage. It can be a very good arrangement because sometimes the mentor writes the person being mentored a cheque at the end of their tenure so that they can set up their own business.

But the onset of the Industrial Revolution, which took root first in Britain during the 18th century, eroded personal relationships among the labouring classes, who moved into the cities and factories in large numbers. Meanwhile, manufacturers gradually reduced wages and rationalised production with the aid of new machinery. The impoverished and alienated working classes were deprived of their old apprenticeships, some of which may have been individually corrupt, like many of those described by Dickens, but nevertheless served them much better than the "depersonalised mass training" described by Clutterbuck in his book *Everyone Needs a Mentor*.

Mentoring did not entirely disappear with industrialisation. Those at the top of large companies kept an eye on promising young recruits, and lower down supervisors might have taken a young apprentice under their wing on an informal basis. This informal relationship, which continues today in many businesses, is not entirely a good thing, argues Clutterbuck, since such relationships are prone to "old-boy networks" that operate by invitation only and exclude and alienate others.

Despite these drawbacks, a group of social scientists at Yale University headed by Daniel J. Levinson studied the lives of 40 influential men in *The Seasons of a Man's Life*, published in 1978. They found that mentoring was one of the most important relationships an individual can have in early adult life:

> The mentor, ordinarily several years older, with greater experience and seniority in the world the protégé is entering, serves variously as teacher, sponsor, adviser and model.

Cultural differences

The type of mentoring practised varies strongly from country to country because of underlying cultural differences, says Dutch writer Geert Hofstede, who devised a framework for studying the interaction of national and organisational cultures. He essentially divided countries into either low or high power distance cultures: the extent to which the less powerful members of institutions and organisations expect and accept that power is distributed unequally.

In low power distance cultures, for example in Austria, Israel, Denmark and New Zealand, people expect power relations to be more equal, consultative and democratic. They relate to each other as equals regardless of their formal positions, and subordinates expect and demand the right to question those in authority. In high power distance cultures – one of the most extreme examples being Malaysia – those in subordinate positions defer to those in power who are more autocratic and paternalistic in approach. They acknowledge and accept the power of others on the basis of where they reside in the hierarchy.

In Europe, power distance is generally lower in northern Europe, particularly in Scandinavian cultures, and higher in southern and eastern Europe. France, for example, is relatively high power distance, says Liz Borredon, an independent consultant at EDHEC, one of France's *grandes écoles*, who has been involved in a number of coaching and mentoring initiatives in both France and Belgium:

> You have to be aware of what the French describe as se dévoiler – to reveal oneself – something that may be at the heart of good coaching or mentoring, but not necessarily something that the French feel entirely comfortable with.

It is not just about whether pouring out your soul is considered good form or not. There is also the issue of power from a French perspective. A mentor might expect to draw out answers from those they are mentoring, but the role of coach or mentor confers, in the eyes of the French, professional status and the assumption that the person in such a position is expected to supply the answers. Borredon says:

> It's not so much a problem, but something which nevertheless can trip up those who are unaware of cultural differences.

Religious affiliation also cuts across this convenient parcelling up of cultures into high and low power distance. For example, in Malaysia the Muslim majority adhere to high power deference, while Malaysian Buddhists are low power.

The United States may be the land of the free and relatively low power when compared with Malaysia or even Japan, but much of corporate America, particularly in its more traditional manifestations, is high power distance. "The hierarchy is biased towards class, money and race – the boss is the boss," says Clutterbuck. That is one of the reasons why what he describes as "sponsorship mentoring" flourishes in the United States.

This is a form of mentoring, he says, where the mentored is protégé (literally "one who is protected"). The mentor is almost always more senior so the learning is generally one way. This type of mentoring, which is commonly used for graduate recruits, can break down with any power shift in the relationship or if the person being mentored is unreceptive or antagonistic to the proffered advice.

It is that sense of inequality at the heart of many mentoring relationships that troubles Helen Colley, who talks of seeing a boy in a school in which she was previously involved being inappropriately hectored and bullied by his wealthy businessman mentor, who she says was placing unrealistic demands and expectations upon the child. Yet the child, as she readily acknowledges, appreciated the relationship and did not wish it to end. There is also a contradiction at the heart of mentoring, she maintains. There is no clarity of consensus about its meaning. Moreover, she says mentoring is devoid of a sound theoretical base on which to underpin policy or practice.

When mentoring fails

A report published in September 2008, *Youth Mentoring: a good thing*, by the Centre for Policy Studies, a right-leaning UK think tank, shares some of Colley's concerns. While good mentoring can undoubtedly help address issues such as social inclusion, says the report's author, Richard Meier, there is little evidence to suggest that it works for all, especially the most disadvantaged. That is because many of the mentors involved in such schemes are inadequately trained to deal with vulnerable young people and some of the projects are ill-conceived and poorly executed. Meier says:

> *What is the rationale for believing that placing an adult with minimal training with a vulnerable young person will be helpful? Government and individual mentoring organisations have to stop claiming that mentoring is some kind of panacea for disaffected youth. It should be recognised as a highly skilled, specific form of intervention for troubled youth and needs to be much more carefully monitored than it is now.*

The Mentoring and Befriending Foundation, a national strategic body that supervises mentoring schemes across the UK, encourages and supports good practice, but there are no statutory requirements for training and supervision, which means quality can vary greatly.

The report gives examples of how such schemes can fall down. One illustrates how a poorly managed mentoring scheme left 15-year-old Ben feeling disillusioned. He was not happy when teachers informed him he was being given a mentor, because of his "anger problems":

> I'd had a couple of fights, what teenager doesn't? I was one of 20 in my year to be chosen, out of 200 kids. I knew there were much worse kids than me. It made me feel like a bad kid.

Nevertheless, he warmed to his mentor, and appreciated having someone to listen. However, things turned sour when he learned she had shared personal information with a colleague:

> The first thing she told me was that it would all remain confidential. After three sessions, I confided in her that things weren't good at home. In the fourth session, she brought a colleague and started going on about getting me into foster care.

The mentoring relationship broke down:

> I was given a mentor because of my so-called anger and it ended up making me feel angrier.

Other horror stories recounted by Meier include one about a 15-year-old pregnant girl, who was given a 20-year-old female mentor, who as a single mother was regarded by the authorities as a "good fit" for the younger girl. However, the mentor clearly had problems of her own, persuaded her young charge to let her move in with her, encouraged her to smoke cannabis and then trashed the girl's flat.

The government's Social Exclusion Unit summed up the situation when it concluded:

> Despite widespread support for mentoring and peer mentoring programmes, the evidence base ... is very patchy and inconclusive.

Even more worryingly, Meier notes that without exception, the young people he interviewed resisted the employment and training outcomes as a focus of the mentoring relationship. They had very different agendas, he says:

> Some sought support for mental health problems or a difficult pregnancy. Others saw mentoring as a space to relax, escape the pressures of their lives, have fun etc.

Although some mentors began by following the guidelines given, they perceived a clash between these and the concerns of those they mentored and usually ended up prioritising the latter, says Meier. He advises that the parents of such people become much more closely aligned with the schemes. He warns:

> The state should not attempt, as the UK Government is doing, to use mentoring as a substitute for parental involvement.

Business mentoring

The lack of appropriate training is also apparent in business mentoring, says David Lester, a successful entrepreneur turned investor based in the UK. A lack of good-quality information for entrepreneurs encouraged him to set up Startups, a web-based organisation designed to offer advice and practical support to small fledgling businesses, which includes mentoring.

Lester, who mentors two or three entrepreneurs in whose companies he has invested, believes mentoring is the poor relation in comparison to coaching:

> There is little in the way of self-help literature and few appropriate training schemes. It is hardly surprising that there are a lot of inexperienced and sometimes not very good mentors around.

In the UK, the Prince's Trust, which helps disadvantaged young people set up their own businesses, gives a limited degree of training to its mentors, says Lester. Public support for small businesses, such as Business Link, varies in quality and often includes former bank managers, who may not necessarily know much about running a small enterprise:

> Coaching entrepreneurs require specific skills. The demand

it places on mentors can be unpredictable and very intense.
Things tend to crop up suddenly. I could not cope with any
more than two or three people to mentor at any given time.

Lester is a former accountant who says he quickly got bored by
number crunching. He became involved with a group of friends
who were running a small computer games company in the late
1980s and decided to invest £10,000 – the money he had saved
to buy his first apartment. It was an astute investment since the
company, which they moved to the United States, was eventually
sold in 1995 for several million dollars. Lester continued to make
investments in other entreprencurial ventures, but he grew increasingly frustrated by the lack of what he describes as good-quality
information.

Entrepreneurs, Lester says, need to be mentored by someone who
has experience of setting up similar operations, which is why mentoring can be so valuable.

Larger organisations can also benefit. Goldman Sachs operates
several mentoring programmes and instituted another in 2008.
It directly involves members of its London-based European management committee, made up of the firm's most senior partners,
in mentoring lower-ranked female managing directors who are
senior in their own right, but who have not so far broken through
to the so-called "golden circle".

The bank is no stranger to such ventures, having already instituted
a number of mentoring schemes in recent years aimed at retaining talent, many of them involving women at associate and vice-
president level. Sally Boyle, who heads Goldman Sachs's Human
Capital Management (HCM) and is a mentored managing director
herself, says:

There are particular challenges in retaining women because of
the domestic challenges they face during some parts of their
career. For a start, women don't have access to the same infor-
mal networks that men tend to take for granted, which can
leave them feeling isolated or even alienated.

This is why the organisation decided to set up a mentoring network
aimed at its more senior women. Boyle explains:

The idea is that we spend time with the senior guys and talk to them about what it's like to be a senior woman in the organisation, but still a minority.

She acknowledges that there is an element of reverse mentoring involved – the most senior men in the firm get first-hand insights into challenges faced by senior women working for the firm.

One of the issues clearly identified by Boyle and others at Goldman Sachs is the propensity of women, even more senior women, to be less proactive when it comes to pursuing their career:

I think women just tend to get their heads down and apply themselves to whatever job they have. Men, on the other hand, are far more direct about seeking out career opportunities for themselves.

A solicitor by background, Boyle was co-head of Goldman Sachs's Employment Law Group before becoming head of HCM for the firm. She says:

I agonised privately for a very long time about whether I could go into such foreign territory and whether I would be playing to my strengths etc.

She compares her initial indecision to that of one of her senior colleagues, who by contrast, when offered similar promotion, immediately set about using his male network to consult 17 colleagues and then accepted.

There are many challenges in setting up such a mentoring scheme, not least finding the time in busy schedules to meet at least four or five times a year as well creating opportunities to shadow senior leaders. While Boyle remains an enthusiastic advocate of mentoring, she does not believe it will necessarily deliver the desired results if it is implemented in overtly hierarchical organisations such as more traditional law firms, for example:

The Goldman Sachs structure is pretty flat and the culture non-patriarchal, we already know most of the top guys since we tend to work with them very closely – I already knew my mentor pretty well.

CASE STUDY

Elizabeth Coffey

American-born Elizabeth Coffey, UK Mentor of the Year in 2007, has been finding her role as adviser to international business leaders more challenging than ever.

In 2009 she said:

I don't think I can ever recall a time like this. There are so many businesses out there under massive threat, losing the trust of their clients and under attack from governments.

While Coffey, who coaches as well as mentors, remains resolutely circumspect about not naming names, it is not hard to realise that she is referring primarily to the challenges faced by many in the financial services industry. This is where she first began to make her mark more than 20 years ago, first informally as the wife of a senior banker and later as a professional coach and mentor.

The climate at the time meant that business leaders were under what Coffey describes as "hellish pressures". Business theories about what exactly constitutes good leadership were cast aside as bosses struggled to keep their companies afloat and possibly themselves out of jail for past actions that may be legal in one country but not in another. She said:

I know of people who are being made redundant as well as people who are actively positioning themselves for redundancy as soon as possible just in case the money runs out before they get paid off.

One of the benefits of a good mentor or coach in such circumstances is to bring what she describes as "the news of the world" into the boardroom. Coffey says:

People tend to get wrapped up in internal politics, which is incredibly prevalent right now, to such an extent that they lose sight of the bigger picture, which can be incredibly dangerous. Part of my job is to shine a mirror on that outside world.

Another aspect of her work is to be a confidante and sounding board for leaders in what is proving to be new and uncharted territory. Much of her workload involving leadership is concentrated on what she describes as "crisis management".

In such an environment, some of the "niceties" of leadership, for instance a more collegiate or interactive style, tend to fly out of the window:

> On tough days you don't always have the luxury of being able to consult others to the extent you might otherwise like to. You have to take actions and sometimes do hard things on your own.

When the dust has settled and the economy has stabilised, there will be irresistible pressure for greater corporate governance and a much greater emphasis placed on risk management, something that global research shows that women are intrinsically better at than men. A Leeds University Business School study in 2009 of some 17,000 companies in the UK suggests that the presence of women on the board can cut the chances of bankruptcy by as much as 20%.

Although Coffey was awarded the title of Mentor of the Year in 2007 by Women of the Future Awards, she has no formal mentoring or coaching qualifications. "I feel quite embarrassed when people ask about my qualifications," she says. However, what Coffey lacks in coach-specific accreditation, she makes up for in hands-on experience. She has worked with chief executives and other board members of FTSE 250 companies for the past 13 years. Her latest book on leadership, 10 Things That Keep CEOs Awake: And How to Put Them to Bed, was published in 2002.

Her own childhood, she feels, was one long preparation for her current role. The daughter of a professor of philosophy, Coffey was brought up in the Socratic tradition, which meant she asked a lot of questions intended to enlighten the recipient. She also had a seriously ill mother, who was an invalid for much of her upbringing, something she believes led to her insatiable urge to "mother" not only her younger siblings, but also others who have subsequently crossed her path:

I would go as far as to say that I've been using the coaching techniques that my father taught me most of my life ... I'm afraid I used to get called the class "shrink" at school.

She may have had little idea back then that what she was naturally practising now constitutes coaching, or even mentoring, but her background was to serve her well. After her marriage she began informally to help her banker husband resolve work problems and then her natural abilities began to be recognised by others within his circle:

I started when I began to advise them about personal problems and then it began to extend to business. All the time I was learning about the banking world.

After a period working as a headhunter, she began to move into organisation development on joining the Change Partnership in London as their first female director. After five years with the organisation, she left to join Mercer Delta to head the firm's leadership practice. After three years doing that she set up her own company, Spark Leadership, in 2005.

What in her view constitutes a good mentor? Coffey believes age and wisdom are vital. "Go back to the original Mentor of Odysseus fame – he's still the best model," she says, referring to research by Andrew Kakabadse at Cranfield School of Management showing that older chairmen have more experience and a manner perceived to work better than that of a younger chairman. Coffey says:

A good mentor has wisdom, a low ego and a determination to ensure that the person they're mentoring succeeds. I think they must also like the person with whom they're working.

She also believes that a good mentor will do what the best coaches do. They may possess content and knowledge as well as invaluable contacts to help their client, but they will not always rush to give advice. Sometimes it is far better, she says, to question and challenge in the same way a good coach will:

When companies set up mentoring schemes internally, you sometimes find some of the more ambitious people rush to try and get mentored by the most senior person in the hope that they will get instant preferment. In my view, sponsorship is not mentoring.

Companies also sometimes fail to pay sufficient attention to the planning of such mentoring schemes, which then leads to disappointment and failure. "I've seen companies rush into this, without working out what the ground rules should be or the expectations and inevitably they fail," she says, adding that internal mentoring schemes should involve initial training for both the mentor and the person being mentored:

One of the difficulties with getting very senior people to be mentors is that they're used to barking out orders most of the time, especially in such time-constrained areas as banking. They say to the mentee, "Look, this is your problem, this is what you do", and end up being surprised when the so-called mentoring relationship doesn't flourish.

Perhaps it is a job best left to professionals. Many businesses slashed their leadership development budgets in late 2007 when the global economy began to experience a slowdown. While many such larger developmental programmes remain dormant, if not dead, many business leaders are quietly seeking help from external mentors like Coffey. She says:

It's all done by immediate need rather than long-term development. If people need critical skills training, in say sales, then those companies will spend money on it. A lot of chief executives have found the going so tough that they're insisting they get some back-up.

Everyone, it seems, could benefit from a mentor, especially in times of trouble.

CASE STUDY

Paddy Murphy

To say that these are challenging times for the airline industry, caught as it is in the eye of the perfect storm, is something of an understatement. Warren Buffett was right when he said that so much money had been lost by the airline industry in his lifetime that perhaps it would have been better if the Wright brothers had never taken off from Kill Devil Hills in 1903.

"The airline industry is like no other industry," concedes Paddy Murphy, one of its veterans, who acknowledges that many of its managers never willingly move on, a tendency that may not be entirely healthy.

The former chairman of low-fare airline Ryanair has moved on, but he has returned to the industry he loves, this time as a professional mentor. Times are exceedingly difficult in the notoriously cyclical industry, which nevertheless gives rise to fierce passions. Much of Murphy's current workload involves trying to chivvy up executives, some close to tears as they fight back the anger and fear they feel at the loss of their jobs. With that curious mixture of Irish empathy and hard-nosed boot-up-the-backside that the newly redundant sometimes need to galvanise themselves into action, Murphy says:

> I've had a few of those and sometimes it's very hard for them to move on. I ask them how they're going to set about proving what a terrible mistake their former employer made.

Now based in Geneva, Switzerland, Murphy continues his aviation consultancy practice as well as his charitable work. But in the past few years he has changed direction since signing up to a coaching course run by The Coaches Training Institute in London, which he says completely altered his outlook:

> I found myself even at my relatively late age pulled completely outside my comfort zone. Consultants come into companies to do a study and then come up with a set of recommendations and then bully their way into doing the implementation.

Coaching, he discovered, does not do any of that. It enables chief executives to find their own solution and stay fully in charge, "which is how it should be," he asserts. Much of what he does as a mentor also involves many of the coaching techniques he learned on his course.

Despite his enthusiasm for the new discipline of coaching, he decided he would not re-badge himself as a coach. Instead he opted to become a professional mentor, which involved very different skills from the ones he previously deployed as an industry consultant.

The one thing the aviation industry does not do is what he describes as the "lovey-dovey stuff", or rather the personal issues that many coaches say you cannot divorce from work. Airline executives generally respect only those who speak the same language, so coming in with detailed aviation knowledge and senior managerial expertise is an essential requirement.

Murphy spent 25 years working for Aer Lingus, Ireland's national airline, where he ended up as head of strategic development, before leaving in 1987 to run a ferry company, Irish Continental Group, trading as Irish Ferries, which floated on the Irish stock exchange a year later and in London in 1993.

As a result of the money he made, he no longer needed to work as a full-time executive, opting instead for a series of non-executive directorships. During this period, Murphy also became involved in a number of charitable schemes in Zimbabwe and South Africa, which after two years he abandoned. "I just couldn't face the corruption that I saw all around me in those countries," he says.

It was during this period that he was approached by a former Aer Lingus colleague, Tony Ryan, who had founded GPA, an aircraft leasing operation. Ryan persuaded Murphy to become non-executive chairman of Ryanair, a heavily loss-making regional airline he co-founded in 1985.

Murphy's tenure coincided with the moment in aviation history when Ryanair was about to finally enjoy its "David" moment against Aer Lingus, which the Irish government was doing its utmost to protect. Deregulation of the skies was finally under way, thanks to the Thatcher government's pro-competition instincts, which opened up the lucrative Dublin–London market to Ryanair from its new base at Stansted Airport. There were 2m passengers a year travelling by ferry between the UK and Ireland who could be expected to switch if air fares came down.

However, it is evident that Ryanair's decision to go for what he describes as "Aer Lingus's jugular" – a battle that is still unresolved – was not one Murphy felt comfortable with. The policy was to get rid of the regional commuter aircraft, not launch an all-out war with Aer Lingus. Murphy says:

> With deregulation opening up Europe in 1993, I felt that we should be concentrating more on Rotterdam and other European operations.

These differences led to his departure from Ryanair. He became an adviser to IATA, an aviation trade organisation, which wanted to become more commercial. His advisory work was given renewed impetus by his decision to learn about coaching techniques in 2005. He says:

> Mentoring is my way of giving something back while being involved in an industry that I love.

3
The coaches

Who are those guys?

Butch Cassidy and the Sundance Kid

Coaches pervade everywhere from boardroom to bedroom, yet they cannot entirely agree on what they actually do.

A rather forlorn American woman is taking part in a free two-day coaching induction course for beginners run by the Coaching Academy in London, the coach training school set up by Jonathan Jay, author of *Sack Your Boss!*, which claims to be the largest in Europe. She wants to lose weight, she explains to the trainee coach, but cannot bring herself to climb onto her rebounder for the desired 15-minute session that she feels would benefit her. "Why is that?" inquires the coach. "Because I don't feel I'm worth it," she responds.

The less skilful person might tell her to get a grip, to get on the wretched contraption and just bounce. But not apparently a coach, who will try to help her sort out her self-esteem issues. And it is not just those who are fighting the flab who feel in need of such services; even high-powered chief executives say it is lonely at the top. Everyone, it seems, needs a coach.

By rights the coaching industry should be in a uniquely happy position. It offers an almost irresistible marketing proposition and one so seductive that only those with the self-assurance of James Bond – or too impecunious to afford the fees – can remain immune to its inherent promise of a more successful, rewarding and happier life. Demand for coaching services, both within and outside the corporate world, has been burgeoning along with their fees, which Jay claims took him from rags to millionaire status.

Coaching started in the corporate arena

When coaching first began to take root within the corporate mainstream a little over 20 years ago, much of its work was seen as predominantly remedial. It was all about "fixing" the more unattractive personality traits of senior executives. As David B. Peterson, a leading North American coach and senior vice-president of leadership consultancy Personnel Decisions International, based in Minneapolis, says:

> Coaching was mainly directed at talented but abrasive executives who were likely to be fired if something didn't change.

Today, it is estimated that only about 10% of the workload of executive coaches involves dealing with "toxic" leaders. Instead the bulk of their work focuses on helping targeted high achievers release further potential. It is conservatively estimated that at least 40% of all chief executives of FTSE 100 companies have used a personal coach, a hired buddy, capable of sharing intimate human vulnerabilities in absolute confidence. More than a quarter of coaches are hired to act as a sounding board, according to a survey published in January 2009 by *Harvard Business Review*, "What Can Coaches Do for You?".

"At senior level people just want their coach to provide them with some 'headspace' room," says Jacqueline Abbot-Deane, a London-based leadership coach and management consultant. Distrust at work means it is not always easy to share problems and ambitions with other senior colleagues.

Moreover, coaching can benefit those who do not have the time and inclination to attend specific business training. By providing feedback and guidance in real time, says Brian Underhill, founder of CoachSource based in California:

> *Coaching develops leaders in the context of their current jobs,*
> *without removing them from their day-to-day responsibilities.*

Coaching may have been largely pioneered by the business world, but it has spread quickly to virtually all aspects of life from divorce, children, happiness, bereavement and career counselling to spiritual and religious matters. There are even coaches who will train you to be a better husband, wife or lover. Coach William Berquist says that the industry is rapidly dividing into different specialities and subgroups, which may bring it into conflict with other professions.

According to a survey conducted by the Chartered Institute of Personnel Development in the UK in 2006, 79% of its corporate respondents claim to be using coaching within their organisations, although confusion remains about what is really meant by the term "coaching", which sometimes turns out to be no more than old-fashioned training under a fancy new name.

The added attraction that coaching holds of helping you deliver on famously good intentions, whether that means turning yourself into the next Mother Teresa or simply becoming really good at your job, is hugely appealing to today's bonused-out, "because I'm worth it" generation, who believe that anything they set their mind to is achievable. And if coaching works even half as well as anecdotal evidence suggests, it must surely be worth a try, or so current business thinking goes.

The coaching industry: size and value

It is hard to find accurate figures about the size and value of the coaching industry. A report produced in 2008 by Pricewaterhouse-Coopers on behalf of the International Coach Federation (ICF), the industry's largest global accreditation agency, conservatively estimates that there are at least 30,000 coaches working in the field – rather than the 50,000 suggested by others – generating worldwide annual revenues of at least $1.5 billion. This is lower than other estimates which put annual coaching income at around $2 billion. According to the same report, the best paid coaches reside in the

UK, where the average annual income from coaching is estimated at $65,136, compared to $53,780 in North America and $50,458 in the rest of Europe.

But these sums, deflated by a generally less well-paid lifestyle and predominantly female coaches, fail to reflect the handsome remuneration of the industry's top practitioners, invariably in the corporate arena. According to a survey of 140 coaches, "The Realities of Executive Coaching", published in 2009 by *Harvard Business Review*, top-tier executive coaches can expect to earn at least $500 per hour, the same rate as that charged by a top psychiatrist in Manhattan. But the same report suggests that some earn up to $3,500 an hour.

One head of organisational development at a major international oil company talked about its raft of top-tier coaches each commanding up to £5,000 ($8,000) a day, a fee that would put them on a par with senior partners at the five top global consultancies. Another London-based coach, who deals only at chief executive level, earns £50,000 ($80,000) a year from each corporate client that he takes on for sessions that last one and a half hours, once or twice a month, and is allegedly in such demand that he has had to turn down prospective clients.

In China, clients can expect to pay between $75 and $2,000 an hour for coaching sessions, depending on the level of coach and client. Veteran coach Eva Wong sourly notes that coaching is not immune from the problems of counterfeiting. Would-be copycats have furtively recorded the training sessions of her company, Top Human, and even ripped off her website "word for word".

But although the pay enjoyed by coaches may fall well below that of their now largely discredited patrons in the financial services sector, it has nevertheless been enough to attract what many established practitioners perceive to be the "the wrong sort" into the fledgling industry. Coaching is a bit like a gold rush, where inadequately qualified and inexperienced people rush in, hoping to make a fast buck. It is ironic that coaches, supposedly adroit at helping others sort out their problems, are bedevilled by failure to weed out the incompetent and fraudulent within their own industry, who are hoodwinking clients, either deliberately or unintentionally, with their half-baked psychobabble.

Economic recession, or even depression, is likely to add to the industry's current woes in that coaches, like just about everyone else, will have to fight harder to protect their earnings. Companies are becoming much more hard-nosed about what they are prepared to fork out, says Peterson:

> *In the last recession companies became much more selective about who got coached and the best coaches continued to be very busy.*

Already there are signs that the market for external coaches is beginning to slow, though there is much greater emphasis on training managers to become internal company coaches. But internal coaches are unlikely to be used for coaching at higher levels of the company.

In theory, the economic downturn should provide an equally welcome opportunity to shake out some of the poorly qualified, bad coaches about whom the rest of the coaching industry ceaselessly complains. But Peterson does not see it that way:

> *I'd like to think that might be the case, but I don't think so, because one of the problems with our industry is that the better coaches are having a hard time differentiating themselves.*

The better coaches, who are capable of reinventing themselves, may seek work elsewhere, while less competent coaches with nowhere else to go will remain.

Directors of human resources departments or with responsibility for the organisational development of big global companies are generally astute about who they select to undertake coaching at board level. But increasingly the process of selection is delegated lower down the ranks, where there may be little experience of quantifying good coaching practice and where pressure to pick the cheapest option is strongest.

Types of coaches

Coaches fall into several areas of expertise and can be crudely categorised into the following hierarchy:

▶ Top "celebrity" coaches, such as Anthony Robbins and Marshall Goldsmith in the United States and Paul McKenna in the UK, whose fees reportedly run into millions and who are extraordinarily good at self-promotion.

▶ The "informers" (described thus by Vikki Brock in her research on the coaching industry) from coaching's early inception in the 1980s as well as its present-day shakers and movers. These are the industry's principal opinion formers who have written about coaching practice, or veterans who have played an active role in establishing recognised accreditation and training programmes within the industry, or even devised or developed coaching methodologies. Coaches in this category include former Harvard tennis coach Tim Gallwey, Sir John Whitmore and Thomas Leonard (founder of the Coach University and the ICF), as well as contemporary figures such as Alain Cardon in France, David Peterson in the United States, Anthony Grant in Australia, Eva Wong in China and David Lane in the UK, who has been strongly associated with the creation of industry standards at the European Mentoring and Coaching Council (EMCC) and the Worldwide Association of Business Coaches (WABC).

▶ High-level coaches, who may not be quite so prominent in the world outside but are nevertheless highly regarded by big global corporations and whose earning power is reportedly large. Coaches in this category include David Fish, John Nicholson (head of Nicholson McBride) and Ian McDermott in the UK, David Rock in Australia and coach psychologist William Berquist in the United States.

What does coaching involve?

What do coaches actually do for their money? Some might say precious little, because the reality is that the person on the receiving end of coaching is the one that does most of the graft. The more cynical would say that as a means of earning a living it is even better than being a management consultant – someone who supposedly asks to borrow your watch when you ask them for the time. But such an assumption ignores the extensive knowledge of psychology and expertise in methodologies for engendering motivation and change in others that most competent coaches need to be expert in to have any credibility.

The coach's job involves working with a client or a group to clarify goals and objectives, and to clarify and define obstacles to their achieving a chosen path or purpose. To do this, the coach must help the client acquire high levels of awareness, self-responsibility and self-belief, because in short, self-belief is the key to most successful human interventions.

There is a great deal of unimaginative, process-driven coaching around. Even those who possess masters' qualifications in the discipline are not necessarily the best in the industry. Some of the best may not have specific coaching qualifications, but they do have an extraordinary ability "to see into men's souls", to get to the very heart of the issue in question, to challenge and enlighten.

But that is just the problem. Some of the best coaches would not get their big toe over the threshold because they do not look the part, argues executive coach James Fulton of Stanton Marris, London-based HR specialists, who as a regular coach for legal firms such as Freshfields is well able to blend into the pin-striped City world:

> The very best coaches have to match rapport, but mismatch impact. So, no, it's not a good idea to turn up in a kaftan and open-toed sandals, you have to look the part.

Sir John Whitmore says:

> In coaching it is paramount that the coachee produces the desired results from the coaching session, without fail. It is incumbent on coaches to understand this and ensure that they have helped the coachee to optimal clarity and commitment to action, including pre-empting all obstacles.

It may sound easy on paper, but given the complexities of the human psyche and the roadblocks that so many organisations have an unerring ability to erect, pulling off all of the above is far more difficult than it would at first appear.

Laura Hayes, a former Goldman Sachs investment banker who retrained as an executive coach, says:

> You can't just roll up and call yourself a coach. And while you don't necessarily have to train as a psychologist, you do need to have a proper awareness of and a fair degree of knowledge of psychology and psychotherapeutic interventions.

Asking what coaches like to describe as "the killer question" – the question that produces the moment of self-enlightenment, or self-awareness, in the recipient – is the coaching holy grail, because without it there can be no effective self-commitment to action.

Marshall Goldsmith (see page 90), a behavioural psychologist and one of America's top executive coaches, talks in his book *What Got You Here Won't Get You There* about an unnamed US Marine Corps general with whom he worked to resolve a specific problem with his behaviour, which was his alienating tendency to be over-judgmental. Goldsmith deployed a "what-if" mind-game that involved the general having to finish the sentence "If I became less judgmental ..." several times over. At the first attempt, the general said the usual predictable, albeit cynical things, such as: "If I became less judgmental, I wouldn't have so much trouble dealing with the clowns at the Pentagon." At the sixth or so attempt, with tears in his eyes, the hard man from the military blurted out: "If I became less judgmental, maybe my children would talk to me again."

But do executive coaches need a thorough knowledge of business? Psychologists and psychotherapists, especially those who have only recently entered the corporate domain, argue that it is not necessary. It is a purist view endorsed by Whitmore.

Others are not convinced. Jacqueline Abbot-Deane believes coaches should be content-free, but not context-free:

> By that I mean you don't have to have been a finance director to coach a finance director. But if you're coming in to work with a CEO on leadership, you need to have some degree of

knowledge about business and some understanding of the type
of challenges that the CEO is facing.

She believes that expert knowledge, in some cases, could undermine the effectiveness of coaching and make someone more of a
mentor than a coach. "You could end up reinforcing something that
clearly needs changing," she warns.

Recent research also suggests that companies are requiring coaching to support business-focused agendas rather than purely personal needs, as has sometimes been the case in the past.

Who works in the industry ...

There is still no agreed knowledge base for coaching. The PricewaterhouseCoopers ICF survey referred to earlier, of more than
5,000 coaches – representing an estimated one-sixth of the global
industry – revealed that 86% have been working in the industry for
less than ten years. The survey also showed that women make up
nearly 70% of the industry. Most coaches – 61% – work part-time,
and again the majority are women. That only four in ten of the
survey respondents coach full time seems to underscore the industry's lack of maturity and permanence.

Furthermore, many coaches are in their 50s or 60s (or older),
having left or at least partially withdrawn from corporate life, or
branched out from other professional disciplines such as psychology, training or sociology to enter the coaching field. According
to PricewaterhouseCoopers, the biggest group comprises people
aged between 46 and 55, and nearly a quarter are aged 56 and over.

Of all the coaching specialities, business coaching remains the most
popular area of activity, with more men than women working in
this arena. Women overwhelmingly concentrate on life coaching,
whereas less than 10% of the men surveyed were involved in personal coaching.

Encouragingly, coaches are usually highly educated. More than half
of those who responded to the PricewaterhouseCoopers survey
had an advanced degree, such as a master's or a PhD. Only one in
eight respondents said they had completed their education before

university, with the vast majority – 88% – holding at least a bachelor's degree.

Other recent research suggests that universities are increasingly becoming involved in coaching research and accreditation.

... and where?

The most mature market for coaching services is North America, where nearly half of the PricewaterhouseCoopers respondents have coached for more than five years. Both the UK and Germany have established markets for coaching. But demand is also booming in other countries, such as Switzerland and South Africa. The BRIC economies of Brazil, Russia, India and China are also showing a strong appetite, largely because of the sheer youthfulness and relative inexperience of many of their managers.

Coaching methods

There is much debate both within and outside the coaching industry about whose method of coaching is best – it is essentially a turf war between those with backgrounds and qualifications in psychology and the rest. According to Peterson, who is also a psychologist, this is entirely the wrong way of looking at the issue:

> I know a lot of fellow psychologists who would make terrible coaches. It really doesn't matter what discipline or background coaches come from just as long as they achieve demonstrable results.

This view is echoed by Catherine Hayes, an expert in organisational development, who has hired coaches for many London-based investment banks and who now advises the UK's National Health Service: "Technique and methodology are less important than a coach's ability to deliver desired outcomes."

In the main coaching is a peculiarly solitary calling, which is both a strength and a weakness: a strength in that it offers individually tailored support to individuals struggling for success in difficult or challenging times; but a weakness in that the industry remains fragmented. Coaches who have built up partnerships within the industry remain curiously unbranded and thus struggle for recognition.

Ram Charan, a high-end *Fortune* 100 coach, says:

> *The coaching industry will remain fragmented until a few partnerships build a brand, collect stellar people, weed out those who are not so good and create a reputation for outstanding work.*

There are simply too many boutiques scattered about the field when what is really needed, Charan says, is the emergence of a coaching leader who can not only define coaching as a profession, but also create a serious grown-up firm in the same way that Marvin Bower did when he invented the modern professional management consultancy McKinsey & Co.

That is likely to remain a tough challenge, says David Brown, chief executive of London-based firm Performance Consultants International, which provides executive coaching and leadership skills to global companies such as IBM, PricewaterhouseCoopers and Procter & Gamble. A former investment banker who used to work for Macquarie Group in Australia, Brown harbours ambitious plans to create many global offshoots of his existing company, which is founded on transpersonal coaching psychology principles, but he is not convinced that management consultancy provides the right role model:

> *I'd certainly like to recreate the same professional diligence and focus as McKinsey, but I'm not sure that management consultancy can ever properly share the coaching mindset.*

It is, he says, rather like giving a man a hammer, then being surprised when he starts looking for a nail. Management consultants always want to "do it" themselves, rather than help and empower others, or rather their clients, to undertake their own joinery. Coaching, particularly when it is at its most powerful, can be quietly subversive of the corporate process, says Brown. The role model in this regard is Warren Buffett at Berkshire Hathaway, who gives managers the trust and freedom to deliver organisational goals in their own way. It requires highly enlightened and courageous leaders to really make it work.

But there are some encouraging signs. Coach pioneer Myles Downey, who founded the School of Coaching in London, one of the UK's first pioneers of executive coach training, agrees that there has been a discernible lack of professionalism around coaching, but believes there are signs this is changing. "We're just beginning to see moves towards proper professional services firms in coaching," he says. Praesta, a London-based international coaching firm, many of whose coaches come from high-level backgrounds in other professions, such as law, accountancy and business, is bringing in the sort of professionalism that Downey says has up until recently been almost wholly lacking.

There are also signs that the industry is beginning to concentrate, forming larger coaching firms or networks rather than loose associations. This is largely a response to the needs of corporate buyers, who increasingly want a wider international reach, says Andrew Lambert of the Corporate Research Forum.

In this respect, management consultancy remains the role model, and many consultancies have repaid the compliment by setting up coaching practices as an adjunct to existing client services. This is a move that is welcomed by Mary Beth O'Neill, a seasoned executive coach, who laments what she regards as the false separation of the two disciplines:

> *I'm concerned that coaching's need to differentiate from consulting is causing unnecessary separation of two incredibly useful tools. They are a powerful combination when used well together.*

CASE STUDY

Sir John Whitmore

Former motor racing driver Sir John Whitmore is one of the coaching industry's early pioneers. Now in his 70s, he has lost none of his crusading fire, particularly when it comes to changing what he regards as the selfish aspects of the modern corporate world, a process that should rightly begin back in the classroom.

The sporting baronet is in his element challenging the conventional wisdom of those in positions of authority. The author of *Coaching for Performance* is giving an induction in the subject to a group of 50 largely receptive head teachers of state-controlled schools in Hertfordshire in his native England.

He asks his audience, whose schools' exam results are among some of the highest in the UK, to recall their own childhoods and to think of an adult – not an immediate family member – on whom they look back with great affection and privately scribble down the qualities they possessed that engendered such fond memories. Surprisingly, the answers are ubiquitous and universal: that person made each feel special, valued and intelligent, treated them as an equal, listened avidly to them, challenged them and believed in them. Above all they made them feel that they could succeed at their chosen task, given their full attention, care, respect and trust. In short, they had just demonstrated the key ingredients of emotional intelligence (EI), which is measured by emotional intelligence quotient or EQ. He demands:

> How come EQ, which has been identified as being as important as IQ – some say twice as important – to one's future success in life and work, is not taught in schools?

How many people in the workforce do you meet who display the same qualities as those of your favourite aunt or grandmother?, he asks.

Many coaches, particularly business coaches, are happy to work within the existing status quo: in other words to use coaching as a means of helping the person being coached climb higher up the career ladder, to attain that coveted pay rise or promotion. Whitmore is not in that camp:

> Coaching is a way of seeing people, don't try and use it just as a tool. If you do, you won't get any real value from it.

In a corporate world obsessed by indicators and measurements of performance and profitability, Whitmore, chairman of Performance Consultants International, an international coaching firm, has had surprisingly little difficulty in commanding a receptive audience among global business leaders. His words, which may sound harsh, appear to have struck a chord with corporate clients. He claims:

> *The economy was invented exclusively for the western mindset. It is inherently hierarchical and currently in the process of breakdown.*

The workplace, he adds, is also an environment of fear, which needs to be challenged. There is another way, an environment of trust.

Conquering fear is something that the former racing driver clearly relishes:

> *Only by helping people liberate themselves from their fears can you unlock the unlimited potential that most individuals possess. That's what a good coach does.*

Fear of failure rather than fear of injury or death is what leads to underperformance on the motor racing circuits and in life generally. He tells of his own brief return to the race track in 1990 after his retirement from motor racing in 1966 and the invaluable lesson learned from his son, who was then five years old. "It was a challenge I couldn't resist," he says. He was asked to drive an 8.4 litre McLaren M8F in which he came a respectable third and second in his first two races. But trouble hit just before the third race – and it wasn't of the mechanical variety. He explains:

> *It was in my head. There I was just too full of adrenalin, I feared not meeting my goal – to win this one.*

Skulking in his hotel room until the last possible moment before going down to the race in an effort to conquer his fear of failure, he was astounded to receive a badly spelt note from his young son. "Bleve in your self," it read. It was a turning point for the sportsman, who went on to win the race.

His move into initially sports coaching – as opposed to traditional sports instruction – followed an influential encounter with Tim

Gallwey (see page 79). Gallwey's big idea that extraneous interference – often the orders given by an overly autocratic coach instructor – interfered with the sophisticated natural mechanisms that the human body has in place to deal with the arguably simple task, found particular resonance with Whitmore, who also suspected that sports coaches would do better to talk less and listen more to their charges.

Gallwey's particular philosophy was centred on the core belief that the biggest obstacle of all to proficiency at sports was the negative thoughts going on within a player's own head. The job of the coach was therefore not to instruct in the traditional sense, thereby complicating matters still further, but to help de-clutter the mind of all such unhelpful thoughts to free the person up to learn naturally.

Whitmore, who claims he has taught golf for 20 years without ever actually playing the game himself, says:

> You don't have to be an expert in a particular field of endeavour to be an effective coach. I don't teach people anything about golf. All I do is help create awareness and self-responsibility in the person being coached. Their own high awareness is their teacher.

Many of the more progressive sports coaches have been influenced by the "inner game", among the UK's top sporting stars none more than Olympic Gold medallist David Hemery. However, the take-up generally has been painfully slow because it requires a major rethink.

"Traditionalists just can't get away from imposing their long accumulated knowledge, which frequently is entirely inappropriate," says Whitmore, who laments that while new technology is adopted at the speed of light, old habits die hard among the sporting fraternity. He believes that this has been reflected in the state of British tennis, which with the exception of Tim Henman and Andy Murray has produced few good players for quite some time. In contrast, New Zealand is well on the way to changing much of its sports coaching to what Whitmore describes as "real coaching".

Like Gallwey's, Whitmore's approach grew out of humanistic philosophy with its essentially optimistic view that mankind can be improved upon by focusing remedially not on what was wrong with it, but rather on its potential. He initially set up the Inner Game skiing and tennis school in Europe before branching out into other fields, particularly business, with the establishment of his coaching company.

Whitmore also realised, like Gallwey, who subsequently wrote *The Inner Game of Business*, that their respective and similar brands of coaching had a much wider application than just sport.

Transpersonal coaching is the next stage of that coaching process, addressing whole systems such as families, schools, institutions and organisations. It also addresses what Whitmore calls "whole person development", which embraces the higher reaches of human aspiration, as well as spiritual development. As the fledgling coaching industry endeavours to impose standards and qualifications on its less-qualified practitioners, he is determined to ensure that transpersonal coaching is included in this.

Whitmore, who believes that such coaching applied to the business world would do much to engender greater social, environmental and economic responsibility, says:

> *Transpersonal coaching is about the qualitative rather than the quantitative. We are knowledgeable but not wise, particularly in our use of technology.*

His mission is to help embed coaching into corporate management culture and link it to the entire training process by creating a team of advanced internal coaches, and by making coaching a key performance indicator as well as part of the return on investment evaluation.

But none of this can work if a company's chief executive does not believe in coaching. Whitmore recalls a series of coaching programmes that he was running for one of the five major UK clearing banks:

> *I insisted on a meeting with the CEO because I needed to tell him to his face that he was wasting his money. You have to*

believe in coaching at the very top of an organisation for it to work. Change at the top, with ongoing support and role modelling, is crucial.

The same is true for his current audience in the UK's educational establishment, with teaching methods that have relied almost exclusively on instilling knowledge into pupils with mixed success rather than unleashing a system that initiates self-learning as well as self-reliance:

We are talking about learning rather than teaching. Once you realise the principles of how people learn you can apply them to youngsters.

Coaching pioneers

Graham Alexander

Born: 1944
Nationality: British

Notable publications
Tales from the Top, Nelson Business, 2005
Supercoaching (with Ben Renshaw), Random House, 2005

Graham Alexander has probably coached more chief executives than any other British-based coach and was one of the first to establish a proper base for executive coaching in the UK with the formation of his London-based firm, the Alexander Corporation. Yet were he to apply for a job as a coach today, when coaching accreditation and qualifications are increasingly coming to the fore, he claims he probably would not get one. He believes that the success he has had and the value he brings derives from the countless hours he has spent coaching individuals and teams over nearly 30 years as well as whatever life and business wisdom he has picked up along the way.

He first became interested in motivation and positive psychology as a manager at IBM in the late 1960s, when he had to run a team of computer operators. "I became passionate about how you get the best out of people," he says. Strongly influenced by some of the humanistic psychologies and eastern religious philosophies that were beginning to make inroads into Europe, he began to run weekend sessions for groups of people who were looking for answers to some of life's day-to-day problems and deeper questions. "I had no formal qualifications to do this," says Alexander, "I simply kept being approached by people to do more of it."

The group sessions gradually gave way to individual coaching sessions and by the late 1970s his strong interest in tennis brought him into contact with Tim Gallwey (see page 74):

> Tim's Inner Game concept did influence me, but it was also a question of confirming that what I was doing was remarkably similar and that I was on the right track.

The sporting analogy was also particularly relevant for corporate clients, he says:

> The Williams' sisters – Venus and Serena – are as good as any female players ever to wield a tennis racket, yet they wouldn't think of performing without the benefit of a coach. Why wouldn't a CEO not want to benefit in the same way from a coach, the outsider who can see opportunities for even better performance?

By the early 1980s it was apparent to Alexander that there was huge potential for coaching in the business world. He worked in this field, gaining a number of high-level global companies as clients, without initially any formal underpinning methodology or framework. It was not until the mid-1980s that one of his clients (a big global strategic consultancy) asked him to come up with one.

The result was the ubiquitous GROW model, which is the cornerstone of most business coaching frameworks, although later coaches have developed variations of the original model:

▶ G stands for goal – for specific coaching sessions and at the end of the assignment.

▶ R stands for reality – where you are currently in your life or situation.

▶ O stands for options.

▶ W stands for wrap-up or the will to take the actions necessary to achieve goals.

Alexander claims his quest was always to maximise performance and fulfilment in people and organisations. The main focus of his work is to enhance individual and collective effectiveness. He uses specific techniques to help senior management understand and address a wide range of issues that relate to high-performance execution of corporate strategy. His particular expertise relates to straddling the domains of strategy, leadership, culture and team or individual effectiveness.

Myles Downey

Born: 1959
Nationality: Irish

Notable publication

Effective Coaching: Lessons from the Coaches' Coach, 3rd edn,
    Texere Publishing, 2003

Myles Downey established the UK's first dedicated executive coach training organisation, The School of Coaching, in London in 1997. Previously those contemplating a career as a heavyweight executive coach in the UK had been forced to seeking training in the United States. Downey trained as an architect in Dublin and might have remained in the profession had his passion for tennis not led him to Tim Gallwey (see next entry).

He recalls, aged 24, coaching a woman in the inner game technique to help improve her backhand. Eight traditional tennis instructors had previously failed to resolve her difficult short, tight arm action. Without telling her what to do, Downey asked her what she could do to overcome her difficulty:

> She mimed the words "bounce and hit" very slowly in perfect rhythm to the ideal motion that she was striving for.

From then on he was hooked on the coaching business, having seen at first hand just how powerful it could be in boosting performance, whether on the sports field or in the boardroom. His early experiences on the tennis court also convinced him to follow a non-directional approach to the discipline. He explains:

The coach is primarily reliant on the resources, the intelligence, creativity and intuition of other people. The coach should get people thinking, not to guide, instruct or suggest, and unfortunately some people who call themselves coaches just cannot do that.

Downey's work has increasingly focused on training people to become coaches as well as coaching corporate clients. Aware of the lack of appropriate training for anyone working in executive coaching in the UK, he established The School of Coaching with The Work Foundation (formerly The Industrial Society) and has to date trained more than 500 business coaches. His corporate clients include the National Health Service, Lloyds TSB and the National Grid.

Tim Gallwey

Born: 1938
Nationality: American

Notable publications
The Inner Game of Tennis, Random House, 1974
The Inner Game of Golf, Random House, 1981
The Inner Game of Work, Random House, 2000

Notable quotation
The greatest efforts in sports come when the mind is as still as a glass lake.

Steve Martin look-alike and former captain of the Harvard University tennis team, Tim Gallwey took a sabbatical in 1971 from his career in higher education and experienced one of those life-defining moments that seem to abound in coaching: he found a job in California as a tennis professional, only to discover he was more of a hindrance to his students than a help:

I realised that many of my teaching instructions were being incorporated in the student's mind as a kind of "command and control" self-dialogue that was significantly interfering with learning and performance.

The former US naval officer had recently learned a meditation technique from the Divine Light Mission's Guru Maharajah Ji, an experience about which he went on record in the *New York Times* in 1973, along with his intention to live in an ashram and practise celibacy. His experience also made him look at his favourite sport in an entirely new way.

He discovered there was too much extraneous mind chatter going on in his students to allow them to fully focus on their game. He began to explore new and non-judgmental methods to help them observe the ball, body and racquet in a way that would heighten learning, performance and enjoyment. The "inner game" takes place within the mind of the player and is played against such obstacles as fear, self-doubt, lapses in focus and limiting concepts or assumptions, he said. The inner game is played to overcome these self-imposed obstacles, which stop an individual or team from fulfilling their potential.

His efforts in this direction culminated in his book *The Inner Game of Tennis*, which described his experiments in detail as well as their surprising results. It unexpectedly ended up on the *New York Times* bestseller list.

A six-part TV series based on the book followed and his principles were applied initially to other sports, such as skiing and golf. The common theme was overcoming self-doubt and fear of failure, which were getting in the way of concentration and enjoyment of the sport in question. There was even an *Inner Game of Music*, which he wrote in 1986 with Barry Green, principal bassist in the Cincinnati Philharmonic Orchestra.

Gallwey's technique, particularly in the golfing arena, brought him into contact with many business leaders, who began to see the implications of inner game concepts and models for bringing about desired changes in their own companies. One of his early clients was telecommunications giant AT&T, which needed help at that time in adjusting to the newly competitive marketplace of the early 1980s. He also worked with IBM:

> *I was asked to help IBM change its prevailing corporate attitude of "we know it all", to that of a learning and coaching organisation.*

Other clients included Apple, which brought Gallwey in to work on its leadership development programme. He also worked with senior executives at Coca-Cola to help them develop the skills that would help the company move towards becoming what he describes as "a learning organisation" – in other words, one capable of adapting to change through the continuous acquisition of learning and knowledge.

Gallwey's work shaped much of the modern coaching movement, including the work of Sir John Whitmore and Graham Alexander, who brought his techniques to Europe and then developed them further.

Thomas Leonard

Born: 1955
Nationality: American

Notable publications

Working Wisdom, Capstone, 1999
The Portable Coach (now retitled *The 28 Laws of Attraction*), Simon & Schuster, 1999
Becoming a Coach: The Coach U Approach, Coach University, 1999
Simply Brilliant, Coach U Press, 1999
The Coaching Forms Book (6th edition), CoachVille (only available to CoachVille members)
The Distinctionary, CoachVille, 2004 (only available to CoachVille members)

If anyone deserves the title of "the father of personal coaching" it is Thomas Leonard, who nevertheless sometimes displayed the dysfunctional tendencies that coaching is intended to iron out. The intensely competitive self-proclaimed master coach toured the United States in a purple RV, emblazoned with the mantra "Success is a Basic Human Right" on the side, but he never managed to achieve his personal goal of becoming as famous as TV diva Oprah Winfrey, whom he credited with making self-help socially acceptable. He died suddenly from a heart attack in 2003 at his home in Phoenix, Arizona, at the age of just 48, leaving a prolific and enduring coaching legacy.

Originally an accountant, Leonard realised that many of his clients were just as interested in life planning as they were in planning their personal finances. He developed a life-planning course, "Life Creates Your Life", in 1988 and then four years later launched the Coach University, or Coach U, based in Steamboat Springs, Colorado, the first organisation to offer formal coach training programmes. A year later he formed the International Coach Federation (ICF), now the world's biggest coaching accreditation agency. He also formed the International Association of Certified Coaches.

Leonard's genius lay in being the first to dissect the various coaching methodologies, theories and principles and rework them into accessible training modules that could be marketed globally. He launched TeleClass.com in 1998, a virtual university with over 20,000 students offering more than 100 classes a week, delivered via conference call. Two years later he and Dave Buck launched CoachVille, which became the world's largest online community of coaches.

David Megginson

Born: 1943
Nationality: British

Notable publications

Making Coaching Work: Creating a Coaching Culture (with David Clutterbuck), CIPD, 2006

Coaching and Mentoring: Theory and Practice (with Bob Garvey and Paul Stokes), Sage Publications, 2009

Further Techniques for Coaching and Mentoring (with David Clutterbuck), Butterworth-Heinemann, 2009

David Megginson's early working experiences were forged in the confrontational world of British post-war industrial labour relations. His first job after university in the mid-1960s involved writing training policies for dock supervisors. It was at a time when ports were paralysed by labour unrest and wildcat strikes. Much of his work was informed by his visits to Tower Hill in London, where he would listen to the oratory of Jack Dash, a communist firebrand and trade union leader, famous for his involvement in

London's dock strikes. He continued to work in the field of organisational development in the steel industry and later at Unilever, before becoming an academic at Sheffield Hallam University, where he was professor of human resource development and is now a visiting professor. Much of his earlier work was influenced by systemic training models developed by the British army but also increasingly by psychology and human motivational theories emerging from such places as the Tavistock Institute in London and the National Training Laboratories in the United States.

On a more personal note, he was profoundly influenced by Roger Harrison, an American management consultant whose work injected a more humane and spiritual element into the business world. The work of organisational development theorist Chris Argyris (see page 11) also resonated strongly with him, particularly Argyris's theory of the "left hand column", which he used to describe the discrepancy between what people think and feel, and what they actually say in their conversations, especially in an environment of fear and distrust. Megginson explains:

> This was brought home to me very forcefully when I was training a leader in an arts organisation. He was so annoyed that his CEO was ignoring his proposals, but he had never actually voiced them, even though he was totally convinced he had done so.

He used coaching techniques in his work and was one of the first to write a book published in 1979 wholly dedicated to its pursuit, *A Manager's Guide to Coaching*, aimed at line managers. He also began to embrace mentoring and joined forces with David Clutterbuck to co-author several books on the subject, including *Techniques for Coaching and Mentoring*, published in 2005 by Elsevier, Butterworth-Heinemann.

Together with other coaching and mentoring pioneers, Sir John Whitmore (see page 71), Julie Hay and Eric Parsloe, Megginson helped form the European Mentoring and Coaching Council, which now has registered members in 18 countries. He also runs masters' degree programmes in coaching under Sheffield Hallam in both the UK and at the University of Applied Science in Olten, Switzerland.

His approach, which has been described as "eclectic" and is based on a variety of coaching and mentoring techniques rather than on adherence to one narrow approach, appeals to the many coaches who have been trained by him, particularly the way in which he has managed to balance practical business considerations with spiritual, emotional and wider intellectual perspectives.

Mary Beth O'Neill

Born: 1953
Nationality: American

Notable publications
Executive Coaching with Backbone and Heart, Jossey-Bass, 2000

Good executive coaches, pronounces Mary Beth O'Neill, must possess the trained yet natural curiosity of a journalist or anthropologist, share their clients' conceptual frameworks, be able to encourage rigour in their clients' thinking and encourage them to extend their competencies by expanding existing knowledge.

But above all, an executive coach must be capable of making the same emotional investment in a client's business as the client does, but avoid, at all costs, becoming mere mirror images of the client's thinking and management style:

> *They must have the strength and courage to face an organisational leader in a time of crisis and speak the unvarnished truth.*

O'Neill, who came to the fore as an executive coach in the 1990s, is a former director of training and development at the Sheraton Seattle Hotel and Towers. She also worked as an external consultant for a variety of American corporations, but turned increasingly to coaching when she realised how much more quickly it helped clients learn, compared with more traditional training methods. She says:

> *I did not set out to become an executive coach; I evolved into one. I was having coaching conversations with executives before it was called coaching.*

She explains that her work in organisation development and

leadership brought her into frequent contact with senior managers. "Sometimes I was sitting with a leader who was disappointed with a project's progress," she recalls. Initially, her lack of experience led her to assume that she and the rest of the team had somehow let him down, but increasingly she realised that the leader's own behaviour was to blame:

> So there I was across from a disgruntled leader. I began to invite him into conversations about his frustrations, asking him what he thought the external causes were and what he might be contributing – though unintentionally – to the slowdown.

Far from this being the recipe for imminent career disaster some might have anticipated, O'Neill has built a strong coaching practice and a sound reputation. She particularly appeals to corporate clients who like their coaching firmly nailed to clear business objectives that can be effectively measured at the end of the project.

Coaches, she asserts in her book *Executive Coaching with Backbone and Heart*, should operate as business partners. They should never:

▶ allow coaching to be regarded as a corporate "finishing school";

▶ undertake an assignment that has no business measures associated with it;

▶ be a substitute for a client's boss;

▶ become a substitute for performance management.

O'Neill is also a senior consultant for the LIOS Consulting Corporation at the Leadership Institute of Seattle at Bastry University, where she runs coaching courses as part of the institution's master's degree programmes.

Unlike some coaches, O'Neill believes that the coaching industry's general need to differentiate itself from management consultancy is misguided:

> It is causing unnecessary separation of two incredibly useful tools which are very powerful when used well together.

Anthony Robbins

Born: 1960
Nationality: American

Notable publication
Awaken the Giant Within, Simon & Schuster, 1991

If ever there was a poster-boy for the self-help movement, it would be Anthony Robbins, with the curiously unreal looks of a Marvel comic superhero. His big message that there is more to each of us than necessarily meets the eye – that everyone has the potential to be amazing – carries universal appeal, though some do not warm to his in-your-face brand of showmanship.

According to *Forbes*, which places the self-proclaimed father of life coaching on its list of the world's 100 most powerful people, Robbins earns some $9m annually from his hallmark programme, "Unleash the Power Within" – four-day seminars that he stages to packed audiences around the world. At least 2,000 people a year complete his life-mastery course at $10,000 a throw, and he earns as much as $300,000 for speeches as well as income from merchandise sales on QVC and infomercials.

He is the living embodiment of the American Dream. In the opening passage of *Awaken the Giant Within*, he recalls the time he flew by helicopter to yet another of his sell-out meetings and spotted the building where 12 years earlier he had worked as a janitor at a time when he was constantly broke, overweight and lonely. It is a seminal moment for the rich, have-it-all millionaire, now living with his wife in a mansion by the sea.

Imagine the life you have always dreamed of living, he exhorts his followers. Imagine there are no barriers or boundaries. Imagine a life rich with success and achievement, endless physical vitality, heartfelt personal relationships and a deep sense of spiritual fulfilment.

A poor boy from a broken home in Los Angeles, Robbins started out selling tickets to other motivational speakers' events, where he quickly gained a reputation as something of a super-salesman. He also became an avid reader of self-help literature, allegedly devouring more than 700 books on the subject. Some of those books led him to neuro-linguistic programming (NLP), which he studied under John Grinder, one of its co-developers, as well as the hypnotherapy techniques of Milton Erickson (see page 15). He later took lessons in fire-walking, which he stages at his various events as a metaphor for overcoming fears and limiting beliefs.

Another facet of Robbins's technique has been his ability to model the actions and behaviour of successful people and develop them into a series of marketable steps for personal goal achievement. He says:

> If you want to be successful, find someone who has achieved the results you want and copy what they do.

Robbins, who also likes to be referred to as a "peak performance consultant", also runs his own corporate coaching company and has worked with several major American corporations, including IBM, AT&T and American Express. He has also undertaken coaching for the US army and, according to Tom Butler-Bowdon in his book 50 Self-help Classics, worked as a private coach to Bill Clinton in the wake of the Monica Lewinsky affair.

Laura Whitworth

Born: 1946
Nationality: American

Notable publication
Co-Active Coaching (with Henry Kinsey-House and Phil Sandahl), Davies-Black Publishing, 1998

Laura Whitworth, who died in 2007 at the age of 59, co-founded in 1992 the Coaches Training Institute, based in San Francisco, California, which claims to be one of the largest coach training schools in the world and the first organisation to be accredited by the ICF. Collegiate in approach, Whitworth's real legacy was her ability to bring coaches together, particularly those who were instrumental in shaping the industry's current direction. She also helped found the Personal Professional Coaches Association (PPCA), the Alliance of Coach Training Organisations (ACTO) and, with Rick Tamlyn, the Bigger Game Company, which originated from her desire to teach coaching skills to prison inmates, a scheme which is still in operation.

Whitworth, who like Thomas Leonard (see page 81) came from a finance background, took up coaching after completing one of Leonard's life-planning courses, "Life Creates Your Life", in 1988. She was also coached by Gallwey for a while and then became involved in Landmark, but found its approach not to her taste. She later told colleagues:

> I did everything I could to make sure that everything I did, didn't look like and sound like Werner Erhard & Associates.

Co-active coaching involves both the coach and the client; it is also referred to as personal/professional coaching because Whitworth, like many coaches, did not believe that professional or work life could be divorced from personal life. Her book *Co-Active Coaching* was essentially written for other coaches and is filled with extensive guidance about how to be effective. It also includes a coach's toolkit comprising forms, checklists, exercises, resources and a glossary.

Coaching focuses on what clients want, she said. People come to coaching because they want things to be different. They are looking for change or they have important goals to reach.

Eva Wong

Nationality: Chinese

Notable publication

The Power of Ren: China's Coaching Phenomenon (with Lawrence Leung), John Wiley, 2006

The formidable Eva Wong claimed in an interview with a Chinese newspaper that she was once just a traditional Hong Kong "woman next door" before finding the personal courage to ditch her 14-year marriage and follow her true path.

It is hard to believe that there was ever anything traditionally submissive about this pioneering executive coach and businesswoman, who has successfully exploited China's phenomenal rise in world economic power and particularly its relative lack of global business expertise. She has also become something of an authority for western businessmen grappling with China's sometimes unfathomable business methods.

Her company, Top Human, spent ten years developing, practising and refining the Ren coaching model. This is essentially a fusion of western management principles, most notably the ideas expounded by American business guru Peter Senge in his book *The Fifth Discipline*, particularly around self-restricting fears, and combining them with Taoist, Confucian and Buddhist beliefs. Much of her book *The Power of Ren* is taken up with case studies that go some way towards explaining China's modern economic miracle. The final part is devoted to a nine-point leadership plan:

1   Passion – those who lack passion and sincerity always retreat in the face of challenge.

2   Commitment requires action, self-discipline, integrity and focus.

3   Self-responsibility – we are usually better at identifying what others, rather than we ourselves, should be responsible for.

4   Appreciation – we need to affirm and cherish others by focusing on their strengths rather than constantly judging them by our own values.

5   Giving without expecting anything back is the path to true happiness.

6   Trust should be self-initiated and fearlessly extended to others.

7   Win-win should be like the smooth collaboration between tango dancers rather than business conducted on the basis of a wrestling match where one ends up winning but both end up hurt.

8   Enrolment is the ability of leaders to touch the hearts of others so that they will be willing to change their behaviour through appropriate action.

9   Possibilities should be like water, or a great river, limitless and allowing for a path of continual learning.

Critics complain that the "how-to" blueprint for delivering such positive change is missing from the book. Nevertheless, *The Power of Ren* serves to illustrate, contrary to popular perceptions in the West, the abilities of modern Chinese business leaders to select the best practice from conventional Anglo-Saxon business models while remaining true to their own cultural traditions and still deliver Wong's win-win ideal.

After the break-up of her first marriage, Wong worked for the Canadian Embassy in China for six years before joining the training industry, where she saw at first hand the ability of training to improve performance, resolve cultural differences and generally improve the quality of life. Four years later in 1995 she established her own corporate coaching firm, Top Human, which has since expanded rapidly within China, the United States, Russia, Europe, Singapore and Malaysia. Her Ren coaching model has been practised and applied by more than 100,000 people, according to an article in *China Today*. A well-known speaker on international business and academic circuits, Wong is on the board of the ICF and currently serves as president of the China Coach Association. She has been elected as one of China's 100 Outstanding Women Entrepreneurs by the China Women's Federation and China Alliance of Women Entrepreneurs.

Wong recently described the rise of coaching as historically significant as the Renaissance in Europe and as "the most innovative and effective management concept this century". It bridges the gap, she says, between human potential and actual performance. She is also involved in a number of community projects, especially those involving young people. She founded the Talent of People Foundation and the Heart Chorus programme, which is active in more than 300 schools in China.

CASE STUDY

Marshall Goldsmith

Marshall Goldsmith is one of the world's top behavioural psychologists, who for the past three decades has acted as a horse-whisperer to those at the top of America's big corporations, namely the testosterone-fuelled Alpha males who invariably dominate them. It is rumoured that Goldsmith is paid about $250,000 a time by each of them.

Forbes has identified him as being among the world's top five business coaches. He has won plaudits from such business leaders as Jean-Pierre Garnier, former CEO of global pharmaceutical company GlaxoSmithKline, Alan Mulally, CEO of the Ford Motor Company, and Mark Tercek, president and CEO of The Nature Conservancy (formerly a managing director at Goldman Sachs), all of whom testify to his talents in helping them to become better at their jobs, and in some cases even better husbands and fathers.

It is all the more surprising, therefore, given the nature of the aggressively can-do environment that permeates so much of America's business culture, that so many negatives emanate from the master coach. The soft-spoken Buddhist from Kentucky, whose client base is essentially confined to CEOs or potential CEO material, asserts:

> *You can't change people who do not want to change or to fix people who think someone else is the problem.*

Goldsmith's break into the nascent coaching industry began 30 years ago with an approach from Paul Hersey, an eminent behavioural scientist, who asked him to stand in for him on a particular coaching assignment. Goldsmith says:

> *I was hooked. I was paid $1,000 for a day's work at a time when I was only making $15,000 a year as a full-time academic. I wanted to do more.*

This led to a further assignment and also a Damascene moment for the fledgling coach:

> *A CEO approached me from a big company and asked me to work with one of his executives, who he described as a real arrogant, stubborn know-it-all. He told me it would be worth a lot of money to him – and to me – if I could fix him, but payment would be conditional on the results. I was given 12 months to turn him around.*

It was the start of a no-win, no-fee system that immediately distinguished Goldsmith, whose assignments typically last anything from 12 to 18 months, in his chosen field. "I'm not there to shoot the breeze with my clients," says Goldsmith, who defends himself from any suggestion that a year, let alone 18 months, is a long time to take over coaching. "One of my clients is on $35m ... his time is worth ten times what mine is worth."

Goldsmith's focus is not so much on the successful habits behind successful people, but rather on curbing unattractive personality traits that may have been holding them back from being even more successful. In his recent bestseller, *What Got You Here Won't Get You There*, he identifies 20 common characteristics that hinder and demean many modern leaders. They include flaws such as:

▶ not listening – an all too common failing;

▶ punishing the messenger;

▶ favouritism;

▶ being judgmental;

▶ making destructive comments;

▶ speaking when angry;

▶ withholding information from colleagues;

▶ intellectual showing off;

▶ the need to win at all costs, even when victory does not matter and may be counter-productive.

Goldsmith does not suggest that CEOs should attempt to fix all their character flaws in one go, but only the one or two that consistently stand out above all others and prevent what he describes as a "nearly great" leader from becoming a great one. The boss's personality flaws are carefully assessed, but not by Goldsmith, one of the pioneers of 360-degree feedback in business leadership programmes, a practice that is now common among coaches. This involves soliciting feedback about a client's behaviour from colleagues at the start of an assignment. In Goldsmith's case, each assignment involves soliciting feedback from a minimum of eight colleagues suggested by the client, and in some cases three times as many.

Readers of Goldsmith's book might be forgiven for imagining that the average American boardroom is a Darwinian nightmare, where inferiors are subjected to foul, abusive language and psychological cruelty. Goldsmith, who also works for global companies in Asia and Europe, disagrees that there is a crisis of manners in corporate America:

> A lot of people ask me that. The coaching industry has grown on the back of everyone's very high expectations of the guy at the top. In the past leadership used to be about a lot of unacceptable things: kings and tyrants who killed people, slavery and sweatshops. I think things are a lot better now and our leaders a lot more sensitive.

The knowledge worker, identified by Peter Drucker, is now ubiquitous. If you shout and scream at your employees, they are likely to seek work elsewhere. Indeed, some of Goldsmith's assignments are triggered when too many of these highly skilled workers, who often possess skills and expertise well beyond those of the leader, decide to depart.

Like the very best coaches, Goldsmith's talent appears to be as much his ability to see into other men's souls as his ability to create self-awareness in his clients. He says his job is to help motivate them into undertaking the work necessary to achieve the desired results that they themselves have set as their goal. "I can only ever be a facilitator in this process," he says.

But it is not just about creating an epiphany in those that he coaches. Many people, with or without the help of a coach, experience profound moments of revelation, but all too often fail to act upon them. "Coaching without follow-up doesn't work," he insists.

"There is a world of difference between understanding what needs to be done and actually doing something about it," he says, citing the number of diet books that consistently dominate America's bestseller lists, while Americans continue to grow ever more obese.

The best stories in his book are the redemptive ones about the invariably hard-nosed, kick-ass types who go on to transform their performance not only in the workplace, but also in their personal lives.

Regulation

*All professions are conspiracies against the
laity.*

George Bernard Shaw

**The coaching industry is striving for professionalism, but it is
finding it hard going as a result of its multi-disciplinary roots.**

The problem is that coaching is not a profession. This annoys most
coaches, especially highly qualified coaches who ply their trade
in the upper echelons of large global organisations. Many would
like the dignity of belonging to a professional body without being
encumbered by the many rules and regulations that govern the
professions of accountancy and law.

If anything, coaches would most like to emulate management
consultants, says Patti McKenna, editor of *The Power of Coaching*.
They would like to assume the same "lawyerly use of rhetorical
language, the handsome remuneration and dignified style of client
interaction". In other words, the blueprint for the coaching industry has been to defend itself wherever possible from perceived
encroachments from other professions and to secure its professional standing through accreditation, while rejecting state regulation and professional liability.

A plethora of coaching programmes

The push for professional respectability is evident in the plethora
of coaching programmes that have sprung up around the globe.

According to Rey Carr, a coach who operates an American website of coaching resources (www.peer.ca/coaching.html), there are 425 coach training programmes in the world, 180 of them associated with colleges and universities. There are many professional coaching bodies and at least nine major ones, the largest of which is the International Coach Federation (ICF).

Despite the proliferation of coaching accreditation programmes and professional industry bodies, there is no "coaching central", no single recognised source or authority, no one governing body, no one standard of certification or licensing. Furthermore, there is no agreement among the varying factions and schools and philosophies about something as simple as a definition of coaching, let alone an agreement over who actually is a coach, or what constitutes good coaching, complains philanthropist Ruth Ann Harnisch of the Institute of Coaching (formerly the Foundation of Coaching). "To quote Gertrude Stein, there is no 'there' there," she says.

University involvement in the certification of coaching is growing, but there are as yet no chairs of coaching in the United States, something that Harnisch would like to address. She has tried repeatedly to endow a chair of coaching, but hitherto with no success:

> A lot of academic institutions are actively discriminating against any attempt to undertake detailed research into coaching. I know of one well-respected researcher who wanted to do a dissertation on this subject, but was told by the head of school that it would be "over my dead body", dismissing it as just so much "American mumbo-jumbo".

In an effort to overcome such hostility, she recently endowed Harvard's McLean Hospital with $2m. As part of that bequest, she stipulated that at least $100,000 should be awarded annually in coaching-related research grants. As Harnisch puts it, "it sends out a message" to the rest of academia:

> It is very interesting that other academic institutions, which had previously tried to steer researchers away from coaching, were only too happy for them to attend Harvard's first coaching conference in September 2008, because Harvard Medical School is so very prestigious.

No requirement for professional qualifications

Despite the glut of training programmes and professional bodies, it is still not obligatory to have any coach-specific professional qualifications, and governments have little desire to address the problem of "cowboy" coaches through regulation.

There are no real barriers to people calling themselves a coach. Since there is no agreed definition of what coaches actually do, and as yet no regulation of the industry, anyone can set up as a coach. This is one reason coaching has grown so swiftly over the past decade. Retired executives, human resources directors, academics and management trainers have been joined by engineers, senior police and army officers, teachers, clinical and occupational psychologists, counsellors, psychotherapists and sportsmen in setting up shop in the coaching industry.

One way of checking whether you are getting a bona-fide coach is to ask whether they have any coaching credentials, says Kay Cannon, a former president of the ICF. But not everyone agrees with this advice. Dave Marchant, a former training manager at WH Smith, a UK retailer, had an extensive background in human resources before starting his coaching practice 18 years ago. He says you do not necessarily need coach training qualifications to be a good coach:

> You do need some key interpersonal skills, broad life and business experience and the knowledge of and confidence to use an appropriate coaching model and approach.

This is a view that Madeline Homan, an accredited coach who heads the Ken Blanchard executive coaching practice in California, has some sympathy with:

> The real acid test is not necessarily whether a coach is accredited, but whether the companies using them retain them and recommend them to others.

Homan, who had a successful career as a Broadway actress before becoming a coach, says she can tell quickly – usually within seven minutes – whether a coach is any good or not:

> *I always make them do a rehearsal for me, before I introduce them to any of our client companies.*

But diversity of background and experience, which Homan and others say is a strength, can sometimes pose problems. There is growing concern that there are too many poorly trained and inexperienced coaches working in the industry, some of whom have never received any coach-specific training or have gained dubious qualifications from the internet or from a short course.

Peter Bluckert, one of the founders of the European Mentoring and Coaching Council (EMCC), says:

> *While there is an important place for introductory programmes, unrealistic expectations can be created by the notion of the one-week "wonder course".*

Most advanced-level coach education is based on the university accreditation model of postgraduate certificate, diploma or full master's programme, taking between one and three years to complete.

Executive coaching competence presumably takes a great deal longer to acquire. But coaches, especially those new to the field and those who want to make a great deal of money, often rush to acquire a specialist "niche" designation within the business coaching arena. Do you work with leaders, top team, high potentials, women, or board members? This is a question that Gill Corkindale, a former *Financial Times* writer turned coach, said she was frequently asked when she first entered the industry seven years ago and which she is still unable to answer honestly now. She writes on her blog:

> *The huge growth in the coaching sector and the lack of regulation have led to individual coaches redefining themselves as specialist "leadership", "development", or "transition" coaches, which are essentially meaningless labels.*

HR directors have colluded in this process, she says, in order, they believe, to match the right coach with the right client:

> *But this is misguided ... real work and development emerges from the relationship between coach and client rather than industry experience or qualifications.*

It is not just coaches within the industry that are worried about lack of standards. Many related professionals, particularly psychologists, have their concerns about coaching, and some of them are canvassing governments to stop what they regard as unqualified practitioners meddling in their field. Worryingly, more than two-thirds of the 500 companies surveyed by UK-based HR consultancy Chiumento in 2007 said there were too many "cowboys" involved in coaching.

This anxiety is already splitting coaching into various subcultures, says Harvard-trained psychologist and coach William Berquist. He warns:

> A coach can work with someone who is anxious, depressed or has ADD, but if a coach is working with someone specifically to address these problems then he is crossing professional boundaries.

The unrestricted use of the term "psychologist" in the UK, write John Passmore and Carla Gibbs in *International Coaching Psychology Review*, "does not help those who have trained for up to five years to achieve a clear and precise standard". In business consulting, they claim it is not uncommon to find people who claim to be "psychologists", when at best they possess only an undergraduate degree in psychology and sometimes little more than training in a level B psychometric instrument. Level B is usually based on four days' training endorsed by the British Psychological Society and supposedly gives people sufficient skills and knowledge to conduct and assess psychometric tests appropriately. The situation in coaching is worse, with limited training available, no regulation and little in the way of licensing.

Does the coaching industry need to be regulated?

It certainly does, if you accept the notion that it is possible to murder someone psychologically. Many companies spend a great deal of money on coaching and it is possible that a bad appraisal of an executive's performance by a hired coach could in theory lead to him or her losing their job. An unethical coach could break confidentiality, going behind the back of the person being coached and reporting what has been said to the sponsoring employer, with highly damaging results.

Such concerns prompted the British Psychological Society to make a formal government application in 2003 to have psychology regulated by the Health Professions Council (HPC), with the result that since mid-2009 anyone practising psychology in the UK now has to be registered with the HPC. This move formally recognises that psychology in the hands of charlatans or incompetent practitioners can have devastating consequences.

Psychotherapy is set to come under the HPC in 2011 and the draft consultation document contains over 450 rules that psychotherapists will have to comply with. The move has sent a chill wind through the coaching industry and some believe it is only a matter of time before coaching gets drawn into the regulatory net. But how would it be done? The very complexity and variety of disciplines and methodologies involved in coaching would make coaching's regulation something of a nightmare for the authorities.

Caroline Horner, who heads the i-coach academy in London and runs coaching masters' programmes in London, New York and Johannesburg, says:

> *Statutory regulation along the lines of that used in psychology and proposed for psychotherapy would be a round peg in a square hole approach at best.*

Jeremy Ridge, chairman of the supervisory panel of the UK-based Association for Professional Executive Coaching and Supervision (APECS), says:

> *I think there's a general feeling in the UK government that business is experienced enough to weed out incompetent coaches.*

Since regulation tends to be done via job title, the very looseness of "coaching" poses significant problems. For example, how would you deal with someone calling himself "a financial coach"? Coaching is not currently regulated, but most financial services are. Ridge says:

> *It's not easy to come up with a sensible framework that actually protects consumers. All too often it degenerates into a box-ticking exercise.*

So far America's coaching industry has successfully fought off efforts by some legislators to bring coaching under the mantle of existing laws governing psychotherapy practice. In Colorado in 2001 officials stated that coaching met their broad definition of psychotherapy, but local coach activists with the help of nationwide coach associations succeeded in having the law amended to expressly exclude coaching.

In Asia to date the field of personal development, including counselling, psychotherapy and coaching, is relatively small. Most coaching is done in the corporate setting and thus already controlled by the corporations themselves.

Anyone who conducts corporate training, education or counselling in China must be licensed, meaning they must pass an exam. But the coaching industry has so far been overlooked. The reality, according to Anne Spaxman of the International Association of Coaching (IAC), is that small operators in any of the above occupations can work unregulated as long as they do not make too much money or create controversy, by being connected to, for example, the outlawed Falun Gong movement, which teaches the ancient technique of self-development built on Taoist and Buddhist principles.

Self-regulation may be the answer

But if the industry is to avoid state regulation, warns Jessica Rolph of the UK's Chartered Institute of Personnel Development, it must press for greater professionalism within its ranks:

> *If pressure is exerted to secure minimum expected standards, qualifications and results, the "cowboy" operators will have no option but to conform.*

It was this desire for appropriate self-regulation that in 2005 brought together four of the major accreditation agencies in the UK – the UK chapter of the ICF, the APECS, the EMCC and the Association of Coaches – to set up their own Round Table, along with coaching psychologists represented by Pauline Willis. Julie Hay, who helped found the EMCC, was also involved:

I think there was a strong desire to see if we could co-operate and harmonise our standards and qualifications.

Progress has been painfully slow, although members remain hopeful that they can reach some form of agreement on standardising regulations covering coaching supervision. But the clarity that the market requires about coaching qualifications and how to go about finding a quality coach is still some way off. Hay believes that standardisation of the industry's various coaching qualifications would do much to address this:

It would be much easier for clients to compare qualifications and work out what is broadly comparable within the various coaching categories.

These issues and the need for wider international co-operation prompted two prominent coaching psychologists, David Lane of Middlesex University in the UK and Michael Cavanagh of Sydney University in Australia, to establish the Global Convention on Coaching (GCC), but whether the initiative can overcome the big egos, professional jealousies and cultural barriers that keep getting in the way of more meaningful collaboration remains to be seen. In their GCC declaration the founders state:

We affirm the immediate imperative for the coaching industry to come together to define and regulate itself.

The purpose of the GCC, which held its first annual convention in Dublin in July 2008, attended by 50 delegates from 16 nations, is to remove boundaries that inhibit dialogue, explains Else Lewis, who heads the standards committee of the EMCC. An indication of just how big a challenge that might be is that the model adopted by the forum is based upon the Mont Fleur process used by the leaders of the opposing factions in South Africa to deal with the aftermath of apartheid, when over the course of a year they held four intensive meetings aimed at envisioning a common future together. The GCC has also adopted the particularly polite form of non-confrontational questioning – appreciative inquiry – developed by David Cooperrider to manage potentially tricky situations where conciliation rather than compromise is needed.

The organisation, which intends to hold further meetings among the 250 people involved in its working groups, aims to:

▶ establish common standards of practice;

▶ produce a universal code of ethics;

▶ produce educational guidelines;

▶ conduct rigorous research into coaching to demonstrate that coaching can help provide new solutions to new and difficult challenges.

There are high hopes for the GCC and the declaration made in Dublin has so far produced 15,000 signatories. But the convention has no structure or formal organisation, and as long as this lack of clarity persists within the industry, one thing is certain: corporate clients will continue to conduct their own beauty contests to select which coaches they want to work for them. Individuals seeking private coaching should do the same on the principle of *caveat emptor* or buyer beware.

The need for caution is further underscored by an ICF survey published in 2004 which revealed that 70% of coaches do not possess professional indemnity insurance. This is something that the ICF has since been working hard to address, and it has devised a comprehensive policy with BW Insurance which covers coaching as well as training, facilitation and consultancy services.

The main coach accreditation or professional agencies

Association for Coaching

Established: 2002
Country of origin: UK
Membership: 2,400 in 34 countries
Address: 66 Church Road, London, W7 1LB
Telephone: +44 (0)20 8852 4854
Website: www.associationforcoaching.com

The Association for Coaching (AC) was founded in 2002 by Katherine Tulpa and Alex Szabo with the slogan "promoting excellence and ethics in coaching". One of the AC's stated aims is to promote greater accountability and credibility within the coaching industry. The original membership was predominantly UK-focused, but the organisation says that it plans to move to a more globally based structure. Its members include not just professional coaches, but also training providers and organisations and companies involved in coaching.

The requirements for accreditation are:

▶ at least three months' full membership of the AC;

▶ evidence of professional indemnity insurance;

▶ a short essay on individual coaching philosophy;

▶ a coaching case study;

▶ references;

▶ evidence of continued professional development;

▶ a minimum of 250 coaching hours;

▶ at least one client testimonial;

▶ a report by a coach mentor or supervisor.

Members have to commit to the AC's code of conduct. Unlike many other coaching bodies, the AC reminds members of their legal responsibilities towards clients; for example, in the area of privacy under the Data Protection Act. It also stipulates that, among other things, members must:

▶ respect professional boundaries by not encroaching, for example, into areas where a client's mental health is a predominant issue;

▶ ensure that clients fully understand the terms of their coaching contract, including fees, number and frequency of sessions;

▶ be open about their coaching techniques and methods prior to the contract agreement;

▶ be sensitive to issues of culture, religion, gender and race;

▶ respect a client's right to terminate coaching at any point;

▶ maintain records of their work with clients and keep any documents securely to prevent third-party disclosure;

▶ monitor their work and seek client feedback;

▶ keep abreast of new laws and rules affecting their work;

▶ consider any potential conflicts of interest in relation to clients or sponsoring organisations;

▶ not act in a manner that could bring coaching into disrepute.

The AC says that it has instigated an efficient complaints procedure, but to date it has not yet resulted in any member being struck off its membership register.

Association for Professional Executive Coaching and Supervision

Established: 2005
Country of origin: UK
Membership: 80
Address: Adam House, 71 Bell Street, Henley-on-Thames, Oxon, RG9 2BD
Telephone: +44 (0)1892 864038
Website: www.apecs.org

The Association for Professional Executive Coaching and Supervision (APECS) may be the smallest of the associations, but it is possibly the most rigorous in the application of its professional standards, although Jeremy Ridge, chairman of APECS's executive coach accreditation panel, baulks at the suggestion that the organisation is in any way "exclusive". It is, however, exclusively focused on executive coaching. It also includes corporate managers of coaching programmes in its membership, some but not all of whom may also be coaches. The organisation, which is based in the UK and is open to overseas members, is not particularly exercised about coaching qualifications and believes that other professional qualifications and relevant experience might be equally if not more relevant. It prefers to keep its distance from the myriad coaching schools and courses which have sprung up like elephant grass in recent years and which tend to seek affiliation with other professional or trade coaching organisations.

Ridge, who believes that some coaching qualifications are too easily acquired without much in the way of intellectual or professional rigour, says:

> I think we feel pretty dissatisfied with much of the training that is taking place within our industry. How many people, once they've handed over their money, actually ever fail their coaching course? I don't think such qualifications should necessarily be taken at face value.

As a result APECS places greater emphasis on its own application form, completion of which is apparently so onerous that the majority of applicants either abandon the process of full accreditation or take six to nine months on average to complete all the various criteria laid down. Candidates must:

▶ demonstrate that their work has involved training individuals at appropriately high levels of leadership within an organisation;

▶ provide evidence of appropriate professional training together with recognised qualifications, such as, for example, British Psychological Society chartered status, or provide evidence of an equivalent level of applied psychological knowledge relevant to executive coaching – this can include proof that they attended relevant courses or followed relevant modules on degree courses in subjects such as sociology, social anthropology, philosophy and neurosciences (appropriate areas of study are likely to include, among others, human development, psychology of motivation and human learning);

▶ provide evidence of continued professional and personal

development appropriate to their involvement in executive coaching.

Applicants who defer full membership may be accepted for associate status, but they must seek full accreditation within five years.

European Coaching Institute

Established: 1999
Country of origin: UK
Membership: not available
Address: PO Box 497, Ashford, Kent, TN24 8WS
Website: www.europeancoachinginstitute.org

The European Coaching Institute (ECI) is the brainchild of South African-born Ben Botes, a management consultant and executive coach specialising in entrepreneurship and small businesses, and Aina Egeberg, a former television presenter turned executive coach, both of whom have since sold out of the organisation. In September 2009, the ECI was to be renamed the International Coaching Institute (ICI) under the continuing presidency of Gerard O'Donovan.

The ECI harbours ambitions to become the industry's main governing body and claims to be the only truly inclusive coaching accreditation agency. Others base accreditation on the core competencies of a few coaching models, states deputy chief executive Barbara Dalpra. But as long as members adhere to the core philosophy, definitions and ethics of the ECI, they should be able to obtain accreditation.

ECI accreditation involves six different levels of experience, based upon training hours and experience. Accreditation applications are carefully vetted along with existing coaching experience, ability and standards.

A code of conduct covers such things as integrity, honesty, transparency and accountability. Coaches must ensure that clients fully understand the coaching agreement, its terms, conditions and costs, and the number of sessions involved. They must not abuse clients' trust or prolong a coaching assignment beyond its useful conclusion, or provide confidential information about a client to employers or others without the client's express permission. The ECI also operates a complaints procedure where clients can register their grievances against coaches or students. The ECI says it has struck off members as a result of previous investigations, but will not provide further details.

European Mentoring and Coaching Council

Established: 2002
Country of origin: UK
Membership: 3,500
Address: PO Box 3154, Marlborough, Wiltshire, SN8 3WD
Telephone: +44 (0)845 123 3720
Website: www.emccouncil.org

The European Mentoring and Coaching Council (EMCC) was founded by Eric Parsloe, who initiated the project, Sir John Whitmore, David Clutterbuck, David Megginson and Julie Hay. Among those invited to the inaugural meeting on October 9th 2002 (and listed among the founder members) are Peter Bluckert, Charles Brook, Alison Carter, Zulfi Hussain, Robin Linnecar, Peter Matthews, Donald McLeod, David Webster and Pauline Willis.

The EMCC says its primary objective is to promote good practice in mentoring and coaching across Europe. The guiding principles are that the organisation should be:

▶ inclusive, for all parties interested in promoting the quality and development of coaching and mentoring, including providers, trainers, researchers and buyers of coaching and mentoring services;

▶ pan-European;

▶ independent, impartial and non-profit-making;

▶ promoting the adoption of quality standards.

Although it was set up originally in the UK (based on a pre-existing association, the EMC), considerable efforts were made to ensure that the EMCC became truly pan-European. New statutes were created and the EMCC was established under Swiss civil law. A Council of Delegates comprises members from various national associations that have chosen to affiliate to the EMCC under a pan-European Council.

By 2006 Hay had replaced Megginson as president and was leading a board made up of members from several countries. Hay was replaced as president in December 2008 by Petr Necas from the Czech Republic and the council now includes delegates from 18 countries.

The principle of inclusivity remains crucial. Anyone can join the EMCC, provided that they agree to abide by the organisation's code of ethics. A policy was approved whereby members in poorer countries such as Bosnia pay less than those in wealthier countries such as the UK. Members are encouraged to establish their own EMCCs in accordance with the legal requirements of their respective countries.

Membership rose to more than 500 by mid-2005, with over 90% based in the UK. At that point, it was agreed that a separate EMCC UK should be set up and by the end of 2008 UK membership stood at 850. Other separate national EMCCs were established in 2005–06 in Sweden, Switzerland, Germany and Turkey and in 2007 in Denmark, the Czech Republic and Ireland. Also in 2007 the AEC (Association Européene de Coaching) became EMCC France and AECL became EMCC Luxembourg (both of these retained their existing names).

During 2008 affiliation agreements were signed with Belgium, Bosnia, Finland, Hungary, Malta, the Netherlands (as an existing association called NOBCO), Serbia, Spain and Turkey. By the end of 2008 the total membership was approaching 3,500.

The EQA (European Quality Award) is an EMCC initiative. It began with a substantial piece of research into the competencies required of coaches and mentors. The EMCC has developed an independent award for providers of coach and mentoring training. This recognises different levels of training and experience and uses a framework whereby programmes are benchmarked against others across Europe.

Two EQA pilot schemes were run in the UK and then formally

launched in 2006, with more pilots following in 2007 in France, Germany, Ireland and Sweden, prior to its launch in 2008. Research is continuing and the EQA will evolve as more is learned. At the same time, there is an emphasis on consistency of standards within member countries.

The Netherlands and Luxembourg retain their own national schemes for individual accreditation. The UK has been developing its own scheme and the launch of a pan-European scheme is planned.

The EMC had been running conferences in the UK for eight years before it became the EMCC. From 2004 the conferences shifted out of the UK, to first Brussels, then Zurich, Cologne, Stockholm, Prague and the Netherlands, with the 2010 conference scheduled to take place in Ireland.

The EMCC produces a regular newsletter and an e-journal, *International Journal of Coaching and Mentoring*. A website has been established comprising a set of pages for the EMCC itself and a series of similar pages for the various national EMCCs, with translations where feasible and necessary. Work in progress to extend the services provided by the EMCC website includes:

▶ a searchable bibliography, with the aim of collating references to all materials related to coach and mentoring so that researchers and others can trace references for selected topics in a variety of languages;

▶ a calendar of events, run by the EMCC and others, so that this becomes the place to look for notification of all relevant events;

▶ a research exchange, where researchers can post details of their research, and later their findings, and others can become involved as appropriate, such as by responding to surveys, being interviewed, and so on;

▶ a professional register that will contain searchable information on individuals and providers, so that potential clients can look for practitioners and practitioner providers (by type of service, location, working language; entries will display qualifications, experience, supervision arrangements) and potential students can check out the availability of training programmes (again by location, working language, and so on).

International Association of Coaching

Established: 2003
Country of origin: United States
Membership: 12,000
E-mail: membership@certifiedcoach.org
Website: www.certifiedcoach.org

The International Association of Coaching (IAC) was established by Thomas Leonard, founder of the Coach U training school, shortly before his death (see page 81). Describing itself as a not-for-profit "business league", the IAC's avowed aim is to raise professional standards through what it describes as a rigorous process of certification. IAC president Angela Spaxman, based in Hong Kong, says that assessment of coaches is based on proficiency rather than on educational background, training or experience. She says the aim is to serve coaching clients in their need to identify proficient coaches rather than the needs of coaches and their desire for credentials and credibility.

The IAC boasts 12,000 members in over 80 countries, with some 65% based in the United States. Given common criticisms that many of the professional certification organisations are too closely allied with commercial training schools, the IAC stresses that the IAC Coaching Masteries programme is "without allegiance" to any training schools or organisations, though it is available under licence to coach trainers and coaching schools. The programme appears to be based upon a series of broad coaching principles such as trust, respect, empathy and lack of judgment, designed to create increased opportunities for the client rather than on any specific methodology. Spaxman explains:

> Our system differs greatly from other systems in that we do not place any requirements on our coaches for how they achieve high coaching standards.

There are three steps to becoming an IAC accredited coach:

▶ Abide by the IAC Code of Ethics.

▶ Pass an online exam covering knowledge of the IAC Coaching Masteries.

▶ Submit two 30-minute recordings of two coaching sessions with two different clients and achieve a passing score as assessed by the IAC Certification Board.

International Coach Federation

Established: 1995
Country of origin: United States
Membership: 16,000
Address: 2365 Harrodsburg Road, Suite A325, Lexington, KY 40504
Telephone: 888 4233131 (toll-free in US); +1 859 2193580
Website: www.coachfederation.org

The International Coach Federation (ICF), the biggest of the industry's various professional associations, was founded in 1995 by Thomas Leonard (see page 81) and a handful of his associates. Their goal was to establish a not-for-profit, professional organisation capable of setting and monitoring coaching standards and ethics across a wide international market. The ICF, which has its headquarters in Lexington, Kentucky, establishes and administers the minimum training standards that individuals and coach training courses must attain before obtaining accreditation. It also generates research into coaching and acts as a network for its members through regional and international conferences. Like many other accreditation agencies in the field of coaching, it also seeks to reinforce coaching as a distinct, self-regulating profession.

Today the ICF boasts about 16,000 members – just over half the estimated number of coaches in the world – in some 90 countries. North Americans make up about 60% of the membership, with Europe and the Middle East accounting for 25%. According to Karen Tweedie, the ICF's president, the organisation remains the industry "gold standard", in terms of both global reach and industry membership, and its implementation of what she describes as a "rigorous" code of ethics. She pledges:

*Any individual who hires one of our members and believes
that something is wrong can file a complaint, which will be
fully investigated.*

All ICF member coaches must sign up to an agreed code of ethics,
which covers all aspects of their practice with client companies
and individuals. The code, which was revised and updated in late
2008, includes client confidentiality, sets out professional boundaries, forbids misrepresentation of qualifications and accreditation,
and bans sexual relations with clients or sponsors.

Past ICF president Kay Cannon advises all potential clients to ask
the following questions, or to follow what she refers to as the three
Cs. Does the coach have:

▶ A code of ethics, and if so, what is it?

▶ Coach-specific training, or appropriate coaching credentials?

▶ Context? For example, if a coach is brought in to coach a senior
executive to undertake complex change management in a bank,
he or she should have the appropriate background or experience
of dealing with such situations.

The ICF does not run its own training programmes, thus avoiding any potential conflicts of interest, but it sets out the training
standards that coaches must attain to achieve ICF accreditation at
three levels:

▶ Associate Certified Coach – requires a minimum of 60 hours of
coach-specific training and 100 hours of client coaching practice,
and successful completion of a written and oral exam.

▶ Professional Certified Coach (for experienced coaches) – requires
a minimum of 125 hours of coach-specific training, a minimum
of 750 coaching experience hours and at least 25 clients, among
other things.

▶ Master Certified Coach (for expert coaches) – requires completion
of a minimum of 2,500 coaching hours and at least 35 clients,
among other things.

So far about 4,000 coaches have gained ICF accreditation since the
programme began a decade ago, which means only a quarter of

the membership has attained what Tweedie describes as the "gold standard", although members may have obtained some form of accreditation elsewhere. According to a recent survey conducted by PricewaterhouseCoopers on behalf of the ICF, 52% of companies say they would require coaches to have some form of professional accreditation.

Despite the relatively low uptake of ICF qualifications, the organisation is determined to raise the professional bar still further and is working towards making its accreditation programmes fully compliant with the International Organisation for Standardisation (ISO). According to Tweedie, this will enable ICF accreditation to gain wider global recognition.

Worldwide Association of Business Coaches

Established: 2002
Country of origin: Canada
Membership: not available
Address: c/o WABC Coaches Inc, Box 215, Saanichton, BC V8M 2C3
Website: www.wabccoaches.com

The Worldwide Association of Business Coaches (WABC) was established in 2002 by Wendy Johnson, a former senior police officer and investigator for the British Columbia government. It also incorporates the former National Association of Business Coaches, a US-based coaching body that Johnson took over in the same year. Johnson's aim is to promote the WABC, which has members predominantly in the United States and Canada, as:

> The world authority on business coaching, with the highest standards of ethics, integrity and professional responsibility.

The WABC offers a number of certification programmes for both individuals and executive coach training colleges or providers. Supervision depends on the level of training programme embarked upon. Basic accreditation is offered through its Certified Business Coach programme, which involves peer review with some degree of supervisor input. More advanced qualifications are on offer through its Chartered Business Coach programme, which lead to accreditation at either chartered or master level. All WABC qualifications must be renewed every five years, a process which the organisation describes as "strict but not onerous". This involves maintaining WABC membership and submitting a record of continuing professional development over the previous five-year period.

The WABC reviewed its code of conduct in 2003 and established a special task force to handle any potential conflicts of interest. With typical American-style hyperbole, it claims to have come up with a code that is "the most unique and advanced ... of its kind in the world today". The organisation says that it has expelled members for breaches of its rules and revoked certifications, but adds that it has had no cause to expel anyone accredited under its more professionally rigorous chartered certification programme.

5 Does coaching work?

If the facts don't fit the theory, change the facts.

Albert Einstein

Coaching has so far failed to come up with convincing evidence (beyond the anecdotal) that it works, let alone provides value for money.

Most people assume and a great deal of anecdotal evidence suggests that good coaching delivers improved performance. Research shows that companies are using more coaching and spending more on it. But how do we know that it really works? Some coaches argue that this is not even a valid question, since so many of coaching's benefits are more qualitative rather than quantitative.

Stratford Sherman and Alyssa Freas wrote in *Harvard Business Review* in 2004:

> When you create a culture of coaching, the result may not be directly measurable in dollars. But we have yet to find a company that can't benefit from more candour, less denial, richer communication, conscious development of talent and disciplined leaders who show compassion for people.

That is all very well, but how do you know coaching can achieve all that if the results of such assessments are not measurable in any convincing way? Do we feel better about ourselves and our jobs after coaching because we demanded it, craved the bespoke attention and status that it confers and are therefore unwilling to admit to ourselves, let alone anyone else, that it might not have made much of a difference – at least not in the long term? It is a bit like spending too much money on cosmetic surgery and then convincing yourself that you look more like supermodel Heidi Klum than the Bride of Wildenstein (a rich divorcee who reputedly spent $3m on cosmetic surgery and ended up looking decidedly bizarre).

This attitude may have been fine in the good old boom days of the economy, but it will not wash in these harsher economic times, says Jack Phillips, who heads the ROI Institute, based in Birmingham, Alabama:

> There is more pressure than ever before on companies to measure the impact of coaching as budgets come under increasing scrutiny. Not all engagements produce the value desired by either the individual being coached or the sponsor who pays for it.

Few companies measure results

According to research published in 2007 by Chiumento, a London-based HR consultancy, it seems that more than two-thirds of the companies using coaching in the UK have yet to respond to such pressures to start measuring. Of the 497 companies surveyed, each averaging about 12,500 employees, two-thirds did not bother measuring return on investment from coaching. The statistics are even worse for American firms, with a survey carried out by management consultancy Hay Group in 2002 showing that under 10% of companies bothered to formally evaluate the results of coaching. Such assessments are just too hard to undertake, or so it would seem.

This view does not cut much ice with David Burnham, founder of Burnham Rosen, a Boston and UK-based consultancy specialising in leadership training, who has spent a lifetime measuring the effectiveness of just such management interventions:

> When HR people have done this in the past, the results have been so poor in the actual percentages of people who change that they now more or less avoid it, relying instead on rhetoric to justify coaching expenditure.

In 2007 Burnham addressed 800 HR directors at an international leadership development conference in New York. He asked his audience if it carried out the standard "Smile" evaluation test after coaching assignments, where people who have completed such courses have to fill out a basic feedback form. There was a unanimous show of hands. He then asked who deployed the tougher level 2 learning and training evaluation technique developed by Donald Kirkpatrick in the 1970s. It involves assessments of skills and knowledge acquired and whether such improvements have been sustained over a certain period – usually six months. This time only 200 raised their hands. He then asked about Kirkpatrick level 3, which involves asking colleagues of the person who has been coached how effective the targeted changes have been. This time there was a show of only 50 hands. Again he asked who deployed Kirkpatrick level 4, which essentially demands that the leader being coached and developed is tracked to see if he or she is performing any better in the business as a result of coaching. Seven people put up their hands.

The exercise was repeated six months later at a similar UK leadership conference, this time attended by around 1,000 HR directors from big UK corporations. The results were almost identical.

This lack of care in tracking the benefits of coaching will have to change. In a more difficult economic climate, procurers of coaching services, like everyone else, will be under intense pressure to show demonstrable results. Without such justification, coaching could well end up being dismissed as a passing fad from the boom days.

Lack of research

One of the reasons the coaching industry is finding it so difficult to justify its own work in this field is the lack of available research, says Caroline Horner of the i-coach academy, which also advises corporate clients about getting value from the coaching process. "The research data is surprisingly hard to find," she acknowledges. She refers to a report by the CIPD, *The Case for Coaching*, published in 2006, which makes a firm case for coaching's effectiveness, but the study is based on only 30 organisations from the UK's public, private and not-for-profit sectors, and can hardly be deemed as substantive or conclusive.

Ultimately, though, executive coaching can be a highly personal experience, so what occurs between the coach and the person being coached is sometimes difficult for companies to monitor. Most business problems are of a personal nature anyway, says an ex-army officer, Jonathan Perks, managing director of boardroom and executive coaching at Penna, a professional services company in London. He nevertheless believes his industry must work harder at demonstrating to clients that it provides value for money. "Proving an adequate return on investment remains the holy grail," he says. But as yet there are no definitive answers, other than for companies to solicit individual feedback from those who have been coached as well as their line managers, and to keep tracking performance and behaviour at various set stages after the coaching has finished, he adds.

Little evidence of return on investment

As long as there remains scant evidence of solid investment return, coaching will remain open to attack. Entrepreneur David Carter, chairman of Merryck & Co, a chief executive mentoring firm with offices in London, New York and Sydney, says:

> Most coaching is a complete waste of company money. It is either a remedial therapy that doesn't stick or work or nothing more than a dissatisfaction industry for those who need a crutch to lean on or who have personal problems that are getting in the way of work.

There is an uncommercial overemphasis on personal matters at the expense of business objectives. "Every such intervention should be able to demonstrate a return on investment of at least ten times the cost," says Carter, whose clients have included Barbara Cassani, an American businesswoman, who he first mentored shortly after the launch of Go, BA's low-cost airline. He then helped her negotiate Go's subsequent management buy-out and a year later the airline's eventual sale to easyJet in 2002. He also mentored John Dunmore, former CEO of brewer Scottish & Newcastle.

Coaching's vulnerability to such criticisms stung the industry into action. A group of 40 people, made up of researchers, coaches and other interested parties, met on the campus of Harvard University in September 2008 in an effort to establish a framework for in-depth academic research into coaching, something that is so far visibly lacking. The resulting International Coaching Research Forum is sponsored by the Coaching and Positive Psychology Initiative of Harvard Medical School, McLean Hospital and the Institute of Coaching, which has pledged more than $2m for individual research projects.

There have been a number of studies on the effectiveness of coaching over the past five years, but much of the work has been limited in scope and the results generally inconclusive. Coaches Annette Fillery-Travis and David Lane, who reviewed such studies in *International Coaching Psychology Review* in April 2006, state:

> What we do know is that virtually everyone likes being coached and believes that their effectiveness or performance is enhanced as a result.

There are particular challenges in adequately measuring the effectiveness of costly external coaching programmes, which still make up around half of all corporate coaching interventions. Traditionally, the person being coached rather than the sponsoring company has defined the coaching agenda, so that often there is no defined return on investment – although there has been a reaction against this. Sponsoring companies are increasingly pushing for more involvement in the contracting phase, usually through involvement with the line manager or HR department.

Both Fillery-Travis and Lane refer to two known studies which were specifically prepared to quote a return on investment (ROI), both of which involve external coaching. The first, undertaken by Right Management Consultants and published by *The Manchester Review* in 2001, gives an ROI of 5.7 in tangible bottom line benefits. However, like many other attempts at proper ROI evaluation, the study is of limited benefit and flawed in that it surveyed the consultancy's own clients and the results were based on the estimates of people being coached. The second, conducted by the ROI

Institute and based on a real but unidentified American international hotel chain, quotes a more modest ROI of 2.21 (see case study on page 124).

But the gap between reality and perception remains. Both of these studies rely on self-reported evidence from the people being coached. Few studies look at assessments by colleagues over the long-term.

In a similar vein, Thatch, an academic, investigated in 2002 the quantitative impact of coaching and 360-degree feedback on the leadership effectiveness of 281 executives within a single company, some of whom took part in more than one of the phases.

▶ Phase one – 57 executives concentrated on 1–3 development actions arising from a 360-degree assessment.

▶ Phase two – 168 executives received four coaching sessions over one year, along with a mini 360-degree assessment and participant survey.

▶ Phase three – 113 executives were given no choice of coach and the coaching was of short duration, although many participants paid for further coaching from their own funds.

However, the assessment was not linked to appraisal and hence the impact of the coaching intervention should have been more clearly defined. Unfortunately, no comparison was made with non-coached executives.

Jack Phillips of the ROI Institute believes that the coaching firms that develop proper evaluation processes will increasingly win business over those that do not. He says:

> First of all, I'm not saying that everything that can be measured should be measured. That is neither desirable nor worthwhile, or that you should use the same set of criteria to measure for every intervention.

But it is sensible to sit down before any such coaching intervention and work out between the client and coach what a successful intervention will look like and how such results can meaningfully be gauged or measured.

Performance improvements may not last

All too often studies have concentrated on the perceptions of the coaching clients, usually through a survey conducted at the end of a specific coaching programme. The response is nearly always unanimously positive, but researchers need to devise something more sophisticated than the original question: "How was it for you?"

Yet another study conducted in 2003 by Harder & Company Community Research, based on the experiences of 24 executives from various companies, reported significant improvements in performance after the coaching sessions. Although follow-up interviews revealed that the benefits were still felt by the executives six months after the programme had finished, this was not sustained when they were assessed again at 12 months.

The suggestion that improvements brought about by coaching may not endure is something that worries Burnham. Indeed, he believes that much of the coaching currently undertaken by organisations may not be delivering the benefits that many imagine:

> Coaching may be good for boosting morale and retaining staff, but I do not believe it has much to do with improving performance, at least not in its present form

This is a view that many might find heretical. But Burnham spent 20 years working closely with David McClelland, an eminent Harvard psychologist, whose original research into social motivation identified three major motives:

▶ achievement – the need to perform well at a given task;

▶ affiliation – the need for friendship and close relationships;

▶ power – the need to exercise it and influence others.

Together the two men set out to discover what sets top-performing business leaders apart from their less successful counterparts – the 15–30% that Daniel Goleman writes about in his book *Working with Emotional Intelligence*, who significantly improve performance, with or without leadership intervention programmes such as coaching.

They began by examining the sales force of an American toy company and discovered that it was inner motivation, rather than behaviour, that distinguished the high performers. They shared the same beliefs and attitudes, and this subtly affected their behaviour. The less successful may have behaved similarly, but they had different beliefs and attitudes and their results were only average.

This pattern was repeated again and again in companies in other sectors. The power motive identified by McClelland was especially dominant in these people. In other words, their inner motivation was to influence others. People who changed, they noted, did not change because of intervention – they improved their performance because they were very much like the people in their organisation who were already high performers. "It was as if the intervention gave them permission to be themselves," explains Burnham.

The interactive leader

So should companies ditch costly coaching interventions and concentrate instead on identifying and fostering the talents of the natural high-flyers to be found within most organisations? Is it the case that companies are spending too much time and money nurturing the wrong people?

It is not as simple as that, says Burnham. His most recent work, based upon the methodology he and McClelland (who died in 1998) applied together, highlights the emergence of a new type of leader who he describes as the "InterActive Leader". This interactive leader derives power from others around him, is collegiate or team-driven in style and good at motivating those around him to achieve common organisational goals. It is the style of leadership typical of a leader such as Barack Obama or even Mahatma Gandhi.

Burnham's research suggests that, rather than being some utopian role model, this type of modern leader is far more adaptable to the furious pace of economic and technological change. The answers to such challenges can no longer be expected to reside with just one charismatic business leader, based on the old institutional business models. The institutional leader saw himself – and it was nearly always a he – as the source of power, explains Burnham.

In support of his theory, Burnham tracked both the qualitative and quantitative performance of 140 business leaders in 18 organisations across eight industries over five years. Although the power motive continued to distinguish the most successful leaders from the others, it was the interactive style of leadership that consistently delivered the most outstanding results, particularly in raising morale, engendering self-responsibility and ensuring that rewards were distributed fairly among the workforce.

But where does this leave the rest of us lesser mortals? The good news is that Burnham believes the inner motivations and thought patterns of these interactive power leaders can be acquired by others. He has trained over 1,000 senior to mid-level leaders in a wide variety of organisations over the past two years and claims to have achieved marked improvements in at least two-thirds of participating and potential leaders.

Although coaching forms part of this change process, its efficacy is linked to motivational training, which takes place over three days, right at the outset of the Burnham Rosen programme. Moreover, a great deal of modern coaching is incapable of delivering the desired result, warns Burnham. Much of its practice is devoted to cognitive behavioural interventions, and as a result much of its efforts are wasted since many of its recipients quickly revert back to type. He says:

> Behavioural training may feel good to the participants as well as the organisations that sponsor it, but research into the actual impact of these efforts often shows that untrained (control) groups do as well as trained groups.

Moreover, the cost–benefit ratio of behavioural training may be negative. Merely acting like a leader rarely produces real and lasting improvements in business results.

So Freud, so despised by the coaching profession for his innate pessimism towards mankind, was right all along. We are all shaped by inner motivations of which we are either ignorant, or at least have a very poor understanding. Not entirely, says Burnham, who argues that individuals can be taught to change the order of their underlying motivations. For example, you might have a leader who has some degree of power motive but an even greater need to be liked by others, which is compromising his or her position. With appropriate training, such motivations can be rewired so that interactive power dominates.

Training to understand and change inner motivation, linked to coaching, is the way forward, argues Burnham:

> Train people to change their inner motivations and you very quickly begin to change their behaviour.

McClelland, Burnham's long-standing mentor and friend, based much of his work on that of a colleague, Henry Murray, a Harvard professor of psychology, who invented the Thematic Apperception Test (TAT), one of the most respected and reliable psychological tests of people's basic needs, which has been tested on more than 60m people. It was also Murray who devised the theory of the three inner motivations – achievement, affiliation and power – that provided the research focus for much of McClelland's own work.

CASE STUDY

Coaching in the hotel industry

One North American international hotel chain insisted that external coaching supported clearly defined business objectives and could demonstrate value for money.

The hotel industry is notoriously tricky, as those running the Nations Hotel Corporation (based on a large North American hotel group the name of which has been changed at the company's request) will tell you. It is ultra-competitive, highly cyclical and price sensitive and you cannot afford to compromise on customer satisfaction. All this places heavy demands on Nation's senior executives, who must, regardless of economic downturn, strive to boost efficiency and revenues.

The US-based chain operates more than 300 hotels in cities all over the world. In 2006 the company decided to coach some of its senior executives, many of whom had been pressing for just such intervention. What was different about this particular coaching intervention was the cautious approach adopted. There was to be no starry-eyed, full-scale embrace of coaching without proper assessment. A pilot scheme was to be launched, involving 25 senior executives at vice-president level and above, all of whom must first volunteer for selection. The senior management team was equally insistent that the intervention must be linked to carefully defined business objectives and that it must demonstrate a clear ROI.

Jack Phillips, chairman of the ROI Institute, which provides evaluation and accountability services to *Fortune* 500 companies, was brought in to help design and monitor the coaching evaluation framework. He says:

> *When you do something like this that has not generally been done before it is better to be ultra-conservative and cautious, but rigorous in your assessment.*

Coaching candidates were carefully selected. They had to be willing not only to be coached and follow through on any planned action, but also to take part in the detailed evaluation that was to accompany the programme. As part of the initiation, each participant provided a self-assessment of their strengths and weaknesses as well as 360-degree assessments by their immediate manager and direct reports.

Nation's learning development team selected a business coaching firm it had worked with before. The roles and responsibilities of each coach and executive were clearly defined, and coaches and executives were paired up on the basis of need and suitability.

One of the biggest priorities was to make sure that the engagement was linked directly to business requirements. As the business consequences of improved performance were identified, they were aligned to specific categories of business needs: productivity, sales, efficiency, direct cost savings, employee retention and customer satisfaction. Outcome targets for the engagement were then connected to corresponding changes in at least three of those business measures. Without such alignment it would have been difficult to evaluate the coaching solution at ROI level.

Individual coaching sessions were conducted at least once a month – usually more frequently – ideally in person, but sometimes by telephone. They comprised goal setting and action planning involving specific action steps to achieve the desired business impact measure. Learning techniques included reading assignments, self-assessment tools, skill practices, video feedback and keeping a journal. After six months, progress would be reviewed.

Fitzpatrick evaluation

Level 1

Participating executives were expected to state whether the coaching was:

▶ relevant to the job;

▶ important in terms of job performance;

▶ effective;

▶ adding value in relation to time and money invested;

▶ something they would recommend to others.

Level 2

Executives were expected to:

▶ identify strengths and weaknesses;

▶ translate feedback into action plans;

▶ involve team members in projects and goals;

▶ communicate effectively;

▶ collaborate with colleagues;

▶ improve personal effectiveness;

▶ enhance leadership skills.

Level 3

This was completed six months after completion of the coaching programme. By then executives should have:

- completed the action plan;
- adjusted the plan accordingly to take account of any market or company changes;
- shown improvements in their ability to identify strengths and weaknesses, translate feedback into action plans, involve team members in projects and goals, and communicate effectively, as well as in their personal effectiveness and leadership skills.

Level 4

After completing the coaching programme, executives should improve at least three specific measures in the following areas:

- sales growth;
- productivity and operational efficiency;
- direct cost reduction;
- retention of key staff members;
- customer satisfaction.

Level 5

The ROI target was 25%. As part of that evaluation it was important to isolate the effects of coaching. Did executives improve because of other factors unrelated to coaching? Here the executives were asked to assess how much of their measurable performance improvements were due to coaching. If they said, for example, that they were 80% certain that improvements in productivity were a result of coaching, the increased value from improved productivity would be adjusted downwards by 20%.

More credible isolation methods, such as control groups and trend analysis, could have been deployed, but they were not appropriate for this situation. Although the estimates were subjective, they were generated by individuals who were best placed to make them – the participating executives.

Wherever possible data were converted using a variety of methods. When standard values were not readily available, estimates from an in-house expert were substituted.

Results of the assessments
Executive reaction to coaching

Relevance of coaching	4.6
Importance of coaching	4.1
Value of coaching	3.9
Effectiveness of coach	3.9
Recommendation to others	4.2

Note: The rating was a scale of 1–5, where 1 = unacceptable and 5 = exceptional

Application

The most important measure of application was the completion of all three action-plan steps, which 83% of the executives reported did; 11% completed one or two action plans.

Executives and coaches also responded to questions about changes in behaviour, some of which are listed below.

Learning from coaching

	Executive rating	Coach rating
Understanding strengths and weaknesses	3.9	4.2
Translating feedback into action plans	3.7	3.9
Involving team members in projects and goals	4.2	3.7
Communicating effectively	4.1	4.2
Collaborating with colleagues	4.0	4.1
Improving personal effectiveness	4.1	4.4
Enhancing leadership skills	4.2	4.3

Note: The rating was a scale of 1–5, where 1 = unacceptable and 5 = exceptional

Application

Translating feedback into action plans	4.2	3.9
Involving team members in projects + goals	4.1	4.2
Communicating more effectively with team	4.3	4.1
Collaborating more with the group + others	4.2	4.2
Applying effective leadership skills	4.1	3.9

Note: The rating was a scale of 1–5, where 1 = no change in the skill and 5 = exceptional

Comments from the participants included:

> It was so helpful to get a fresh, unique point of view of my action plan. The coaching experience opened my eyes to significant things I was missing.

> After spending u great deal of time trying to get my coach to understand my dilemma, I felt that more effort went into this than I expected.

> We got stuck in a rut on one issue, and I couldn't get out. My coach was somewhat distracted, and I never felt we were on the same page.

Return on investment

The coaching fee for all 25 executives was $480,000, which rose to $579,800 once administration, travel, accommodation and other expenses were included. All direct and indirect expenses were taken into account, including time away from work for the executives involved. This was set against identified savings of $1.9m which the participants estimated coaching had generated. Using the total monetary benefits and total cost of the programme, two ROI calculations can be developed. The first is the benefit–cost ratio (BCR), which is the ratio of the monetary benefits divided by the costs:

$$\frac{\$1,861,158}{\$579,800}$$

BCR $= 3.21$

This value suggests that for every dollar invested, $3.21 was returned. The ROI formula for investments in training, coaching, or any other human performance intervention is calculated in the same way as for other types of investments: earnings divided by investment. For this coaching solution, the ROI was calculated as follows:

$$\text{ROI (\%)} = \frac{\$1,861,158}{\$579,800} \times 100 = 221\%$$

In other words, for every dollar invested in the coaching programme, the invested dollar was returned and another $1.21 was generated. In this case, the ROI far exceeded the 25% target.

Intangibles

There were also intangible benefits identified through feedback and questionnaires. These included better commitment, better teamwork, better job satisfaction, and improved customer service and communication. These perceived benefits were included only if they had been identified by at least four of the 25 executives.

Conclusion

For the credibility of the ROI exercise, data were taken from records that could be audited. The executives had no reason to be biased in their judgments and were not responsible for all the data generated. Data collection was handled conservatively by making the assumption that an unresponsive individual had achieved no improvement. (Three executives failed to return completed action plans.) The analysis was also deliberately conservative. Only the first year's benefits were included, when most of the really significant improvements would have been generated in the second and third years.

How to pick the right coach

The best way to find a coach is to seek word-of-mouth recommendations and pursue the hiring techniques used by some of the world's major companies.

There are many good coaches around, but few great ones. There are also many mediocre ones and some who are very bad indeed, warns David Peterson, one of coaching's prominent American practitioners.

Many are refugees, or even rejects, spat out by a corporate system that they wish to return to, possibly fighting back an urge to exact some form of revenge. Some are laden with coaching qualifications or accreditation, but may not have the business expertise to really understand the environment in which they find themselves. Others may have years of professional and business experience but may be too wedded to tired old formulas and business models that failed to deliver in the past and are unlikely to do anything positive now. With fees for an executive coach averaging $500 an hour according to *Harvard Business Review*, it is small wonder that so many companies are paying more attention to the process of hiring the right coach.

A difficult task

It is a far from easy task. Inexperienced companies sometimes delegate it to equally inexperienced people in human resources who often hire the most expensive coach on the basis that price is invariably synonymous with quality. If their bosses turn out to be unhappy with the selection, they can always use the time-honoured excuse that they simply went out "and hired the best that money could buy".

Conversely, the sudden ubiquity of coaching and the desire of some companies to disseminate it more widely to include those lower in the hierarchy mean that the hiring process may be devolved to those further down the command chain, to people who are more focused on keeping costs down than on quality.

Peterson worries that while there are HR people who are extremely skilled in buying in coaching services, the process of hiring is increasingly being handed down to more junior people. He says:

> A lot of people used to buy IBM in the old days, and now we know they opt for the cheapest solution.

Alan Weiss, author of *Million Dollar Consulting*, who has written many books with the apparently noble objective of bolstering the consultancy industry's earning power, would certainly not advocate anyone responsible for hiring returning to the boss and boasting about selecting the cheapest option.

Beauty parades

It is clear, however, that few global companies rely solely on coaching's main accreditation or professional organisations for coach approval. Coach-specific qualifications may be a sign of professional diligence, but they cannot be regarded as a substitute for wider professional experience. Many of the big global companies are not relying on coaching industry standards, but rather staging their own beauty parades to determine who among the coaching community should graduate to their respective approved suppliers' lists. It is a process that many of the most experienced coaches detest.

HSBC, a large international bank, redesigned its coaching selection process in late 2008 after which it held a beauty contest, involving, it says, interviews with over 200 coaches, to come up with its own preferred supplier shortlist. Candidates who did not make it, unlike pupils who fail to get into the best schools, were given their own report card about why and where they had failed, which was "incredibly helpful", says one stoical cast-off.

This apparently time-consuming approach is perfectly justified, says Liz Dimmock, in charge of coaching and development at HSBC. She told the Corporate Research Forum in October 2008:

> I think the organisation should be close to the coach for the best results. HSBC's system is to develop a pool of excellent coaches with a range of skills, and to know their specialisms. We don't believe in box ticking – it's about getting to know individual coaches and their styles. It's then a question of allowing coaches to use their professional skills to identify with those they are to coach, what the detailed needs are, and to meet them.

Thus using a formal assessment process had been "incredibly valuable", she says:

> Coaches may look good on the surface, but we have delved deep into their motivations and observed them undertaking coaching. This really identified who is good.

One of South Africa's largest financial institutions, Standard Bank Group (SGB), embarked on a similar exercise in 2005. Allowing local business units to make their own coaching and mentoring choices had led to a hit and miss approach. Helena Dolny, who then headed the bank's coaching and mentoring unit, says:

> We decided to introduce a screening process to create a pool of "accredited" coaches that any business unit could have confidence in.

Like HSBC, SGB decided early on not to hire just one coaching company or to favour one coaching methodology. It did lay down minimal criteria for years of coaching experience at executive level as well as evidence of continued professional development and supervision. It also made it clear that coaches would be expected to engage with line managers.

The initial impetus for this change goes back as far as 2000, when Standard Bank successfully fended off a hostile bid from a smaller rival, Nedcor. Although the bank had managed to hang on to its independence, the damage had been done. It was portrayed as old-fashioned and intransigent. This prompted the bank to undertake leadership development assessments, which merely confirmed the unflattering picture.

In 2004 and 2005, the bank slipped down the list in South Africa's "Best Company to Work for Survey", something that the organisation realised it urgently needed to address if it wished to remain an employer of choice. At the same time, the bank wanted to fast track the careers of young black managers to challenge the apartheid legacy, thus fulfilling the pledges it had made in the 2003 Financial Sector Charter.

While Standard Bank, like HSBC, pulled the coaching selection process in-house, it also relied heavily on the services of i-coach, a specialist in coaching practice development, based in London, New York and Johannesburg, to help it impose discipline on its scatter-gun approach to the hiring process. Much of the details of that process can be found on the i-coach academy website (www.i-coachacademy.com).

The selection process is growing more sophisticated in most big companies. Senior executives who want to bring in their own choice of coach are increasingly being persuaded to use a more methodical procurement process, based on a disciplined assessment procedure which matches individual personal development with core company goals. At Unilever, for example, a strict assessment is done before coaches are included in a global preferred supplier list. Each coach is expected to have a meeting with a supervisor after every four coaching sessions.

McDonald's: a cautious approach

While finding the best coaches for its leadership development programme is also paramount at McDonald's, a fast-food retailer, staging beauty parades is not something the company is keen to embark on. In the UK, for example, it relies on its coaching partner, Penna, to come up with a list of suitably vetted coaches appropriate to the company's requirements. Jez Langhorn, head of talent and education at McDonald's, explains:

> We still vet our coaches ourselves, but we do so from a rela-
> tively small pool supplied to us by our coaching partner. We
> make sure that the selected group closely matches our goals and
> culture. Many of them are former business people.

The company's talent planning processes are not widely broadcast and coaching is not something that is automatically included.
Langhorn says:

> Coaching at McDonald's tends to be used to enhance per-
> formance, and is rarely used for remedial purposes. It is not
> something that you can nominate yourself for and is generally
> reserved for high potentials. Everything on this front has to be
> approved by our [UK] board.

McDonald's is also busy revamping its restaurants and its menus
with healthier options. It is keen to cast off traditional perceptions
of a brash and overly American approach to its global business.
Coaches must also be equipped to deal with emotional intelligence, the so-called "soft" interpersonal skills that McDonald's
senior management are keen to foster. Emotional intelligence
testing now forms a core plank of the assessments undertaken as
part of any coaching assignment.

But how does McDonald's make its final selection from the relatively small pool of coaches that Penna presents? Experience is
important, says Langhorn:

> Penna will not consider anyone for coaching assignments
> who has less than five years of experience. Authority, pres-
> ence, impact and the ability to fit into the company's culture
> are all important. Grey hair is a good sign. So too is pace and
> enthusiasm.

That cautious and selective approach to coaching is endorsed by
Cisco Systems, the world's biggest provider of net gear, primarily
the routers and switches that drive traffic over the internet. "Coaching is just one tool for executive development," says Charlie Johnston, HR director for the UK and Ireland. Between 30% and 40% of
the company's senior executives are offered coaching – principally
those who are being promoted to new roles, where new skills may
need to be acquired, or to handle some sort of company change.

GE: cautious about outsiders

General Electric (GE) is even more cautious about bringing in coaches from outside. Coaching generally plays a more limited role in the American financial and industrial conglomerate than in most other US-based global companies, according to Susan Peters, GE's vice-president, executive development, and chief learning officer. It is used sparingly. "We are cautious about our use of outsiders," she says. Coaching is sporadic and is usually linked to specific needs. "There are a few exceptions, like Marshall Goldsmith, who we have used." The company also has close links with Vijay Govindarajan, professor of international business and director of Tuck School of Business's Centre for Global Leadership, who coaches executives on business strategy.

The emphasis at GE is on the development of whole teams, which can at the highest leadership levels involve an intensive training programme for no more than 20 senior managers of a specific business area. This is typically undertaken at GE's own management development centre at Crotonville, New York. For example, in 2009 a team of 19 senior managers from GE's power business recently went through this leadership, innovation and growth programme as part of the company's efforts to accelerate its push into new emerging markets, revamp older products and grow new businesses. A detailed account of this appeared in *Harvard Business Review* in January 2009. Peters asks:

> *Should you really be outsourcing the most critical aspect of management, which is your leadership development, to people who might not really understand your culture?*

GE invests heavily in development training, which is very much part of former chief executive Jack Welch's legacy. But while other companies have shifted towards a greater emphasis on strengths, something that GE does not disregard, the company nevertheless remains ruthlessly wedded to developmental needs. Those developmental needs change continuously, Peters argues, so that getting what she describes as the "right domain expertise" is critical to the success of the business.

It all boils down to how you define coaching, says Peters. GE has developed its own internal culture of continuous learning and improvement, which is at the heart of coaching. So too is the company's wholehearted embracing of feedback appraisals, a process that has been formalised throughout the company and applies to everyone including the chairman and chief executive. "We are a feedback culture – here at GE people get it for real," says Peters.

While GE remains unabashed about its self-confessed "macho" culture, involved as it is in the industries of power generation, financial services and health care, others such as Standard Bank look to coaching to soften theirs.

Standard Bank: a points system

The selection process at Standard Bank begins with an electronic questionnaire, which provides basic quantitative information. This is followed up by a telephone interview to determine the coach's process, relationship to the client, preference for certain coaching assignments and any ethical dilemmas.

After an initial screening, coaches are invited to attend an assessment day where they are split into several teams of three and asked to prepare a coaching demonstration based upon a real issue in front of three Standard Bank assessors. Helena Dolny says:

> By interacting with the coaches and watching them at work, we were able to assess their performance against key criteria and indicators that i-coach academy had developed.

For each criterion, the bank drew up a list of positive aspects of individual coaching performance:

▶ Coach and client look relaxed and at ease.

▶ Coach sets up session by making explicit ground rules covering confidentiality, time boundaries, where they can help and when they cannot, and agrees ways of working with the client.

▶ Coach undertakes review of client's current position.

The following negative aspects were also considered:

▶ Coach talks too much, interrupts and finishes client's sentences.

▶ Use of negative body language – crossed arms, looking at watch.

▶ Assumption of meaning without bothering to clarify language.

▶ Disregard for client agenda.

▶ Terminating the session abruptly.

Using a points system, individual coaches were allocated a total score, with the final total divided by the number of criteria. This process was to prove overly cumbersome, however, with around 300 questionnaires needing to be processed in the first 18 months. It was taxing to observe and record accurately. Furthermore, some of the criteria laid down proved less relevant than others and the results generally produced an undesirable divergence in scores.

A number of revisions were made and greater emphasis was placed on the coaches' presentational abilities in terms of insight, self-awareness, engagement and boundary management, and ability to build rapport, handle ambiguity, handle emotions, identify issues and so on. The bank tried out the revised assessment process in London in 2007, and it was agreed that it was easier to run than the original and that there was less variance between assessors than previously experienced.

While undoubtedly time-consuming to operate, even in its more streamlined form, both the bank and the coaches involved have said the process offers clear benefits. Despite anxiety about being so publicly on trial, the coaches said that observing the presentations and practices of other coaches has been an invaluable exercise. Those being coached say that the screening process gives them confidence in an unregulated environment that they have been provided with consistently high-quality coaches. Also, by not selecting coaches from just one company, the assessors have had to engage with a wide variety of coaching methods and techniques; this has been thought-provoking and has added to their existing knowledge.

It is also considered worthwhile by those involved in running the scheme, despite the time commitment involved. Dolny says:

> When we consider whether it has all been worth it, the answer is a resounding yes. We've empowered ourselves as

professionally as we know how, in order to provide a process that's clear and transparent.

Cisco: evaluation of ROI

In an increasingly penny-pinching world, others are taking a harder look at coaching and insisting on some form of concrete demonstration that is delivering real value. Cisco Systems is relatively unusual in its insistence on some form of evaluation of the return on investment (ROI). Johnston says:

> *We also discuss the ROI implications right at the outset: what do we want to achieve, how will we recognise that achievement when it's reached as well as how we should record and measure the impact.*

It is essential that everyone – the company, the person being coached and the coach – agree upon objectives as well as the methods being deployed to get feedback:

> *We build in regular checkpoints along the way to make sure that everything is running to plan, which is really important, since Cisco globally spends a considerable amount of money on coaching.*

At Cisco executive coaching, in tune with the practice of many global companies, is offered to its "high potentials" as part of management leadership development. It does operate mentoring at lower levels within the company and a reverse mentoring scheme, which involves each member of the executive team having a reverse mentor from its team of young graduates. The aim is to help the company's top decision-makers understand the demands and thinking of "generation Y" – essentially young people who were born between 1980 and 2000 and who are now entering the workforce and Cisco's marketplace as potential customers.

But when there are no formal coaching or mentoring schemes immediately on offer for those at middle management level, self-coaching – when individuals and teams take a do-it-yourself approach and set their own goals and objectives – can provide a powerful method of building more effective teams, argues Ged

Fitton, a senior manager of systems engineering at Cisco, based in the UK. He leads a team of 19 engineers, who he says do the "exciting, clever bit", which is providing services and solutions to companies such as BT, Cable & Wireless and the BBC, along with other service providers. The business world is in a state of flux and changing at a pace that is disconcerting, he says:

> Anyone who wants to sell into these particular markets needs to be fully appreciative of those changes. We have to enter into the psyche of our customers and make sure our technology is keeping pace with everything that they're going through.

The big challenge is knowing how to deal effectively with virtual organisations, where individuals can play a pivotal role in the way business is conducted and where customers expect instant answers. In this environment coaching is hugely beneficial, says Fitton. "It is all too easy to run around like a headless chicken ignoring what is critically important." But much of the coaching undertaken in his department is self-taught, although he plans to acquire professional certification from the Chartered Institute of Personnel Development (CIPD).

It is people at middle management level who most need coaching support, he argues. These are the front-line managers who are the oil that makes the whole business machine run smoothly. The process of mentoring or coaching the team has been driven by the high level of talent that the company has been able to attract. Says Fitton:

> We are a company at the centre of and contributing to change, so we tend to be a magnet for talent, which is not the case in businesses that are more transactional.

Self-coaching is a process that complements but also goes beyond the standard HR principles of employee performance management that are laid down as part of the annual review. Fitton's team is exposed to new ideas and practices that encourage it to think differently and challenge the existing status quo:

> There is more risk in this approach because there is less certainty, so you must put the necessary safety barriers – or

> *governance framework – in place. But by going through this process, you find little diamonds of inspiration.*

Cisco has now changed the way it harnesses innovative ideas, or as one executive put it, "Cisco has innovated innovation". Through its iZone Project, the company asked employees to share ideas about new products and services Cisco could offer. Over the course of 18 months, 400 ideas were submitted, which were eventually narrowed to just nine. Three of these ultimately went into production and collectively represent over $3 billion in market opportunity.

"Initiatives like iZone allow us to do things differently," says Fitton. In a company that has grown rapidly and now has more than 60,000 employees, they also act as a healthy bulwark against the tendency to grow too corporate in outlook:

> *I burn at least one day a month getting my team together to develop new ideas and ways of doing things collaboratively. A lot of the things we do involve helping our customers connect to other people with whom they can collaborate as well. The old-fashioned manager who tends to stick to the old ways of doing things is a diminishing breed.*

In a flat organisation, you still need your commanders, the people who supply the vision and leadership. But vigorous effort needs to be made to connect people together, which is where coaching, or self-coaching, as in Fitton's case, can play an important role:

> *You need to allow people to be individually productive in teams that are properly nurtured in a collaborative environment. When you do this, the coaching happens automatically.*

Checklist

So what should companies or individuals planning to engage in coaching do? The list below is based on advice given by many of the world's top coaches and, more importantly, by the people who employ them:

▶ Determine what you want the coaching to do and make sure your objective is realistic and genuinely relevant to the wider business.

▶ Match the person being coached with the most appropriate coach for their specific needs and make sure they can work well together.

▶ Make sure the coach explains his or her way of working and the methodologies employed and that the person being coached is comfortable with the process.

▶ Develop some measures so that you will be able to recognise success when it happens.

▶ Make sure that all parties involved agree to the target, define upfront how it will be achieved and make sure outcomes are part of the coaching contract.

▶ Allow for interim reviews to provide flexibility and a change of direction, if necessary.

▶ Agree the length of a coaching assignment, and how many times the coach and the person they are coaching meet as well as how and where.

▶ Respect confidentiality, but ensure sufficient feedback from relevant colleagues and leaders and develop an appropriate return on investment model for the assignment with input from business leaders outside HR.

▶ Check if the coach has specific coaching qualifications and training, but experience in other fields can be as, if not more, valuable.

▶ Ask the coaches if they are undergoing any form of supervision by a more experienced coach or an accreditation agency.

▶ Check coaches' references and talk to people they have worked with.

▶ Most coaches offer a free introductory meeting which can give a prospective client time to assess whether they feel comfortable with the coach and his or her way of working.

▶ Find out if the coach has signed up to any specific code of ethics, but more importantly ask them to explain in detail precisely what the code actually means to them.

Coaching and mentoring women

*I have yet to hear a man ask for advice on how
to combine marriage and a career.*

Gloria Steinem

**Can coaching or mentoring do anything to help more women
gain board positions, even those who have already fallen off
the corporate perch?**

"I am a product of great mentors, great coaching," says the formidable Indra Nooyi, the 54-year-old chief executive of PepsiCo,
who says she would not have made it to the top of one of the
world's largest food and beverage companies if it had not been for
her mentors, all of whom she acknowledges were men. Perhaps
less well-known is Nooyi's other secret weapon – her mother –
who along with her understanding husband unstintingly helped
raise her two daughters, allowing her to pursue her successful but
demanding career.

Nooyi, a graduate of Yale University, has said in previous interviews that she has always regarded herself as her family's primary
care provider, yet in a speech to an audience at Cornell University
she reveals just how hard it must have been to balance her family's
needs with those of her job.

She recounts how one of her mentors, Steve Reinemund, her
predecessor as CEO and then president of the company, asked
her to go to Frito-Lay, the company's snacks division, in Texas to
reorganise its direct store delivery system, at a time when she was

heavily engaged in the company's corporate office in New York. His request imposed something of a dilemma:

> What Steve was saying to me is you need detailed direct store delivery experience, which only Frito-Lay has, and you need to go get that experience to move ahead in the company.

As a result she spent four days a week commuting to Dallas before returning to do her normal job, which she condensed into just three days by working on Fridays, Saturdays and Sundays. She acknowledges that it involved a "great investment" – not sacrifice – of her time. Her mentor with his challenge had nevertheless provided her, as she recalls, with "a great step up the corporate ladder".

Conflicting demands

Nooyi's story will no doubt strike a chord with many women struggling to meet the demands of career, home and children. For the majority of these women, life is often a series of uncomfortable compromises as well as conflicting and sometimes exhausting demands, especially if they do not have access to the same kind of supportive family network that Nooyi's traditional Indian upbringing provided.

Younger female high-fliers are more willing to talk about the demands of corporate life – but only up to a point. Carol Bartz, the new chief executive of Yahoo!, says:

> Women have more of a burden on them to manage the house and manage the children and manage the school interface.

Bartz says that she made every effort to see her daughter, who is now 20, every day when she was younger, but that sometimes parental involvement took second place.

Why women drop out

The reality is that most high-powered men have stay-at-home wives. Three-quarters of senior male executives who report directly to the CEO or are responsible for large groups of people at some of the world's biggest US-based global companies said their wives did not work, according to a survey sponsored by IBM, "Leaders in a Global Economy", published in 2003. Yet the same three-year study showed that 74% of women business leaders interviewed had husbands or partners who worked full time.

It is not something they teach at Harvard Business School, but one of the best career choices for clever and ambitious women remains, as it always has been, marriage to a wealthy man. This is confirmed by the surprisingly large number of women with Harvard MBAS who drop out of the workforce.

A study in 2008 by UC Berkeley's Haas Business School, *Opt-Out Patterns Across Careers: Labour Force Participation Rates Among Highly Educated Mothers*, suggests that these Harvard business graduates are more likely to become stay-at-home mothers than female doctors or lawyers. Catherine Wolfram, an associate professor at Haas who led the research, based the study on 1,000 female Harvard alumni. She suggests that the business world is less female-friendly than medicine and law. By the time they are 15 years out of college, 28% of the Harvard women who went on to get their MBAS were stay-at-home mothers, compared with only 6% of women who obtained medical degrees. The study also looked at the career paths of Harvard women who became lawyers and found that 21% chose to stay home with their children.

Men who are in the upper ranks of their profession with stay-at-home wives earn 30% more than men who are married to women who work, says Joan Williams, director of the Centre for WorkLife Law at the University of California. Those men who want to reach the highest rungs of their career and earn the most money need a stay-at-home wife to take care of all other aspects of their life, including raising a family. Williams says:

> And since many women in business school marry those men, they end up being stay-at-home wives, regardless of their own vision of what they wanted from their careers.

As a career choice, it is not without risk. The recession is killing off the trophy wife, *Tatler* magazine trumpeted in 2008, referring to the SUHS phenomenon – the "suddenly useless husband syndrome", the alpha male who has lost his high-paying job along with the glossy lifestyle that his money used to support.

Women kept out of senior posts

Futurist Patrick Dixon, author of *Building a Better Business*, talks of the pressing need to attack what he sees as a male conspiracy to drive women out of senior positions in organisations. At a University College London Institute for Women's Health conference held in London in 2008, he referred to the phenomenon of "toxic testosterone" conspiring to drive women out of their rightful place in the boardroom.

That is because the working environment is designed by men for men, who find it much easier, as a result, to align their work values and goals, says international consultancy Catalyst, which looks at issues related to women. As a result women are more likely to find:

▶ less access to challenging jobs;

▶ less supportive workplace cultures;

▶ a poorer fit between home and work;

▶ fewer opportunities for high achievement and higher pay.

This view is endorsed by research conducted in 2008 by the Institute for Employment Studies and published in a report, *Encouraging Women into Senior Management Positions: How Coaching Can Help*, on behalf of the Institute of Coaching. Andrea Broughton, one of the report's co-authors, says:

> Despite decades-old anti-discrimination legislation, women are still under-represented in a wide variety of industries, especially at higher levels. We found remarkable parallels in the experiences of women across the globe, and of the barriers to career progression at board level.

Factors both inside and outside work were found to hinder the organisational progress of women, including male-dominated networking groups and childcare issues.

Furthermore, women who are not driven out of top posts earn less than their male counterparts, according to a survey of executive pay of 3,242 North American companies, published in 2008 by Corporate Library. Female CEOs earned more in base pay, but when cash bonuses, perks and share compensation schemes were included, women made a median $1.7m, or 85% of what the male CEOs made.

Where does all this leave less educated women, or women in general? In an even weaker position. Fewer women at the top of companies means fewer female role models and the prospect of little change in the male-dominated status quo. This is made worse by the preference among companies to appoint either sitting or retired male chief executives to their boards. Herminia Ibarra, a professor at INSEAD, an international business school with campuses in Singapore and Fontainebleau, France, says:

> A sitting CEO is perceived to have great value because he or she is facing the same issues and complexities at their own companies. The number of women is restrained by the small number of people who have reached that level.

Gender inequality

Chairman Mao said women held up half the sky, but not, it seems, when it comes to the corporate world. And as a result of the global financial crisis, more women than men are likely to lose their jobs in 2009, especially in areas such as Latin America and parts of the Caribbean, according to research by the International Labour Organisation.

In its annual report, *Global Employment Trends for Women*, the Geneva-based organisation said that up to 22m women could join the ranks of the unemployed in 2009. While women account for just over one-third of the global workforce, or 1.2 billion out of a total of 3 billion people, the global unemployment rate for women was likely to reach 7.4% compared to 7% for men. Juan Somavia, director-general of the UN agency, who also acknowledges women's lower earnings and lack of social protection, says:

> Gender inequality in the world of work has long been with us, but it is likely that it will be exacerbated by the crisis.

Life is not much better in the UK. In 2008 the government's equality watchdog expressed concern that the number of women in the UK's most powerful positions was falling as they hit a "reinforced concrete ceiling" of discrimination, particularly in areas such as politics, the judiciary and policing, compared with five years earlier.

Though the findings of the UK's Equality and Human Rights Commission show that the number of women directors of FTSE 100 companies had increased marginally from 10.4% to 11%, the report also highlighted "old-fashioned ways of working" by many employers, with bosses still yearning for the good old days when men were the breadwinners and most women stay-at-home mothers. A survey by the European Union showed that men earned on average 17.4% more than women and in the UK 21%.

By contrast, Norway's centre-left coalition government has enacted positive discrimination legislation to force companies to place more women on the boards of the country's largest 500 publicly listed companies in the private sector as well as state-owned enterprises. All such companies are now obliged to have at least 40% women on their boards, which has already lifted representation of women from 7% in 2006 to more than 21% in 2009.

If the Social Democrats regain power in Sweden, similar moves could be implemented, says party spokesman Claes Borgström. Swedish women control 24% of the seats on the boards of Sweden's largest 20 companies, according to a recent study by the Swedish parliament. But there is a wide discrepancy. For example, Swedbank has equal representation between men and women on its board, followed by retailer H&M with 43%, but electronic giant ABB has no women on its board. The incumbent centre-right coalition government, however, while allegedly keen to address the inequality, is not in favour of affirmative action, believing that it would lead to another type of inequality.

Although Sweden usually ranks close to the top globally in matters of gender equality, a new study by Företagarna, published in 2008, reveals an exception in the country's number of female entrepreneurs, which is lower than almost every other country in Europe.

The study reports that only 3.9% of Swedish women run their own companies, well below the EU average of 5.7%. Anna-Stina Nordmark Nilsson, chief executive of Företagarna, says:

> The results are alarming. Things look pretty bad when it comes to gender equality among entrepreneurs, from both a national and international perspective.

Only Malta and Ireland received lower gender equality rankings than Sweden for entrepreneurs, according to the study's comparison of 25 EU member states.

In Spain, the Socialist-dominated parliament has passed legislation calling for 40% board participation by women by 2015, but so far lacks the enforcement measures that accompany the Norwegian law.

In the Netherlands, TopBrainstorm, a pressure group, has come up with a voluntary charter that will set targets for women to obtain more board positions, which it hopes it can persuade companies to sign up to.

Can coaching and mentoring help?

What if anything can coaching or mentoring do to address such challenges? Quite a lot, says Ruth Ann Harnisch of the Institute of Coaching, which is based at Harvard Medical School's teaching faculty, McLean Hospital:

> My own scalp still smarts from crashing into the glass ceiling repeatedly. I am always looking for tools that can dismantle the obstacles to anyone's ability to grow, contribute, and shine. Coaching can make a difference.

A recent report, *Encouraging Women into Senior Management Positions*, commissioned by the Institute of Coaching, finds that effective coaching can help women in a number of areas such as confidence, coping with a new executive role, identifying values and goals, balancing work and life, and identifying what is personally important to them.

But for coaching to have any lasting impact on working women's lives, it should also involve men. Harnisch says:

If coaching is really going to make a difference to women in leadership, then you also have to coach the men as well to think differently about how they do things.

The fact that so many of the traditional leadership models seem to be failing may present an historic opportunity for change. Jeff Imelt, chief executive of GE, says:

The economic crisis that's going on right now doesn't represent a cycle, it represents a reset. And people that understand that will prosper and people who don't understand that will get left behind ... When we come out of this fog, this notion that companies need to stand for something and need to be accountable for more than just the money they earn will be profound.

That new paradigm may involve an increasing recognition of the value and experience that women can bring to companies. Krister Svensson of Brussels-based CMi, a mentoring programme set up to help newly appointed directors and chief executives, says:

If you have 12 grey-haired men average age 65 on a board, they tend to think about business prospects and strategy from the same perspective. But if you put a 45-year-old from a hot company and a woman and an international representative on the board, the quality of the debate will deepen.

Women need to be tougher

But until that happens to a much greater extent than is the case now, women will just have to fall back on traditional coping tactics. Psychologist and coach Lois Frankel, author of *Nice Girls Don't Get the Corner Office*, accuses women of wimping out of the perennial war of the sexes. They need to toughen up if they are going to survive in the corporate world, which she likens to a game of tennis:

It's a game where all the rules are devised by men, so you have to play like them in order to win.

That means hitting those hard, mean shots to the outer limits of the court, rather than always playing it safely in the middle, which is what most women tend to do, she adds.

The lack of women in top leadership positions is to do with the way girls are raised, says Frankel, who was a former occupational psychologist with oil company Arco, now part of BP.

It doesn't matter whether we are talking about baby-boomers, generation x or y, they still face the same old problems. They're brought up to be care givers, rather than CEOs.

Her advice is to speak up at business meetings. Too many women are retiring violets when it comes to pushing themselves forward to express views, says Frankel:

Women wait to be asked their opinion and the chances are that the meeting ends and they haven't said anything. Move in after the first speaker and that way you will avoid appearing too aggressive.

Also, she adds, do not be afraid to sit next to the most powerful person in the room, something she says that many women instinctively shy away from. She also urges women to stop expressing their opinions indirectly through a question:

Women do this instinctively to soften the message, but you just end up being overlooked. If you want to be taken seriously express your opinion as a statement.

But in case anyone reading this mistakenly assumes Frankel is urging women to adopt the toughness of Rosa Klebb, a ruthless Russian agent in one of Ian Fleming's James Bond novels, *From Russia with Love*, she warns females not to emulate their male bosses and thus risk being stereotyped as "the office bitch". American businesswoman Martha Stewart is seen as too pushy, but Sherry Lansing, former CEO of Paramount, Meg Whitman, former CEO of eBay, and Golda Meir, former Israeli prime minister, are role models who meet with Frankel's approval.

Despite all her talk of toughness, Frankel notes that leadership style is changing and softening, something she describes as the "feminisation" of leadership, a trend that might actually help more women achieve more seniority in the workplace:

We've had a hierarchical style of leadership for centuries and we now know that it no longer works, in fact it's totally discredited.

American-born Kate Grussing, managing director of Sapphire Partners, a recruitment consultancy based in London specialising in the placement of senior professionals, believes that something much more radical needs to happen if more women are to assume high-level positions:

> I think we need to think about positive action, not affirmative action, as being the best way forward. I don't think the Anglo-Saxon mindset will readily tolerate legislation to impose women in senior positions.

Grussing, who was a Wall Street investment banker and a management consultant at McKinsey & Co before setting up her own business, undertook a survey in 2008 of women in the workplace. Surprisingly, many of the 407 respondents – many of them in the so-called marzipan layer of middle management – did not regard coaching as relevant, not because they did not believe in it, but because they generally had little access to it.

She urges employers to use coaching and mentoring to address the issues surrounding female advancement. She also believes women need more help in the planning of their careers since they often lack the vision and confidence required:

> I think there are real dangers of women going off-ramp: of accepting jobs that look like promotion, but actually aren't. They are not going for the stretched assignments that would put them in line for the more senior posts.

The real worry, says Grussing, herself the mother of four young children, is that women who take time out for childcare or for a new relationship are finding it extremely hard, if not impossible, to get back into the workplace. The chances are that even short breaks away from corporate life end up being highly detrimental.

Mentoring may be more effective ...

Perhaps the most effective tactic for office survival, especially at higher executive levels, is mentoring. A small study conducted by

Judi Marshall of Bath University in the UK of female managers from middle-management to director level revealed that 70% were either in, or had previously had, a mentoring relationship. All placed considerable importance on the relationship and agreed it had been important in their career development.

Women generally find it much harder to gain the same range of experiences and career opportunities as men. The old boys' club also makes it much harder for women to enjoy the same networking opportunities as men. Those women who do break into the informal magic inner circle are often regarded by the men as unwelcome interlopers, or with suspicious malevolence by female colleagues. "What did she do to get there?" is the usual remark. No amount of legislation has been able to overcome these invisible barriers.

Low expectations or stereotyped images can mean women managers are delegated to undemanding jobs, says David Clutterbuck, author of *Everyone Needs a Mentor*. Women are expected to perform tasks that are essentially seen as suitably feminine, such as personnel, rather than more masculine roles, such as financial analysis.

This view is endorsed by Sue Clarke, a professional mentor and coach who works for the Fiona Harrold Consultancy in London:

> *Men in general are more competitive than women, so it's difficult for female managers to confide in male colleagues.*

Coaching and mentoring offer them some support in the workplace, says Clarke, who undertakes both executive and life coaching.

Five years ago, most of her predominantly female clients wanted to talk just about their careers and how they could use coaching to gain promotion, but they are now increasingly looking beyond the corporate environment for their solutions. "My older clients are especially stressed out, everything in the workplace is much more aggressive," she says.

But younger clients are also seeking more of a balance in their lives. Clarke, who when interviewed was coaching a pregnant Italian woman who works for a management consultancy and is expected to work hard up to her due date, says:

> *I detect a huge backlash against corporate life, women want to have families and are not prepared, unlike some of the baby-boomers before them, to delay or even deny themselves the opportunities to have children because of work.*

But not all her clients share this disparaging view of the modern workplace. She coaches many women from eastern Europe, who are, she says, exceptionally well motivated towards work and career advancement to the extent that many of them are rejecting traditional values involving marriage and children.

Male–female mentoring can be highly effective, says Clutterbuck, in that such a relationship can influence both the formal and informal networks of an organisation. A conventional structured career plan aimed at women managers can yield only marginal benefits since it cannot influence the invisible social network. However, a formal mentoring relationship:

▶ provides a woman with legitimate access to male executives who have the power to influence her career – an informal approach to a male executive could be seen as sexually provocative;

▶ increases her visibility within an organisation;

▶ provides legitimacy through her mentor's public gesture of support;

▶ allows less inhibited interactions with a male superior ideally in a sexually neutral environment.

... but there can be drawbacks

But there can be drawbacks. A woman cannot always fully emulate her male mentor and may have a very different style of operating. For example, a woman may deal with conflict in a less confrontational manner than most men, and this could be seen by her mentor as a lack of assertiveness or confidence.

There can also be sexual tensions and the very existence of the relationship can give rise to rumours and innuendo. A big age disparity between a mentor and his protégé can sometimes lead to the mentor being overprotective, which can create dependency and unwillingness for the relationship to end on both sides.

The high visibility that such relationships sometimes attract means that many mentors are reluctant to take on a protégé. One leadership development adviser says:

A young man may be allowed to fail quietly and then move on, but a woman in similar position is subject to endless gossip.

Clarke believes the benefits of mentoring far outweigh any downsides:

Lots of big companies are now introducing formal mentoring networks and a lot of women are keen to take advantage of them.

However, she also believes that such relationships are not that highly valued by those higher up the hierarchy:

It's not always valued in the way that it should be, which is part of the short-sightedness that afflicts modern working culture.

CASE STUDY

Temituokpe Esisi

On the face of it, Temituokpe Esisi is an unlikely client of Goldman Sachs. In 2008, the 33-year-old Nigerian law graduate turned fashion designer was ready to shut up shop after three tempestuous years. Her fledgling business, with just six employees, was winning plaudits, but was not making money.

That was when a family member spotted an advert in a local newspaper and encouraged the despairing entrepreneur to apply for a course at the Pan African University of Nigeria, specifically set up for women like her. It was the first of many that are currently under way at universities throughout the developing world, thanks to a $100m donation by American investment bank Goldman Sachs, which made profits in 2007 of $11.4 billion. As part of the bank's scheme to help women like her in the developing world, not only did she gain access to top African business expertise, but also her own personal mentor, Michelle Pinggera, managing director at

Goldman Sachs and chief operating officer for the European securities division.

"Initially it was all very intimidating," says Esisi, whose business is now on a sounder footing and may even go global, an outcome she attributes in no small part to her mentor's involvement:

> *Designing was my passion but I didn't know much about running a business – in fact I was doing it all wrong.*

Goldman's 10,000 Women – the number of female entrepreneurs the firm plans to put through five-year programmes similar to the one embarked on by Esisi – was launched on March 5th 2008 in New York. New academic partnerships were announced amid considerable fanfare at its London headquarters, ironically on the blackest of Black Mondays, September 15th 2008, as global stock markets plummeted on news of Lehman Brothers' bankruptcy and deepening global financial crisis.

The scheme – the bank's largest ever philanthropic commitment – remains part of what CEO Lloyd Blankfein describes as its policy of "enlightened self-interest". The idea is that its 10,000 women entrepreneurs will go out and mentor other women in their respective countries to succeed in business. It is hoped that the 10,000 may swell to 10m, many of whom one day might become clients of the bank. To make sure that happens, Goldman Sachs is working with the Bridgespan Group, a non-profit organisation that helps charitable foundations to optimise social impact. The aim is to devise an appropriate structure with which to measure that intended impact.

It is still early days, but Esisi is already actively mentoring her own team of largely illiterate tailors by helping them learn to read and write. She says:

> *So what if they go off and set up in rivalry to me. That would be great – there's room for competition.*

Enlightened self-interest also enables Goldman Sachs to benefit nearer to home. By allowing its own staff to participate directly in 10,000 Women, it helps them play a more involved role in supporting communities, something that helps attract and retain talented people. The company recently invited employees to attend an internal mentoring information session expecting 200 to show up, and was amazed when 700 of them piled into a cramped auditorium.

While Goldman Sachs Europe remains in the *Times* newspaper's top ten list of favourite graduate employers in the UK, the firm was overtaken in the 2008 rankings by Teach First, a non-governmental organisation committed to persuading some of the UK's most high-flying graduates to teach in some of the worst-performing inner city schools. Jim O'Neill, the company's chief global economist and a committed philanthropist in his own right, says:

> We need to make sure that we remain high up on the list of preferred employers. We cannot afford to be complacent.

The business case for 10,000 Women is a compelling one. Greater emphasis on female education in the BRIC economies as well as in the rest of the developing world could drive up per head income by a further 40% more than the current baseline prediction by 2030, according to O'Neill:

> If world GDP does better because of better female education then, all things being equal, Goldman Sachs will do better.

Although 200m women have entered the global workforce in the last decade, bringing female workers to about 46% of the total labour force, fewer than two out of ten women receive a formal wage in regions such as sub-Saharan Africa. Lack of educational opportunity imposes life-long poverty and higher fertility and mortality rates on such societies. This is compounded by the lack of business and management courses available to women.

According to the International Centre for Research on Women, accessible high-quality business and management training is essential for women entrepreneurs to lead and develop their businesses beyond micro and small enterprise levels and for them to take on managerial roles in larger companies. Goldman Sachs's money will fund the lacking but crucial business and management training by forging a series of global partnerships between universities in the developing world and some of the most prestigious business schools, including Harvard, Wharton, Saïd (Oxford), Judge (Cambridge) and INSEAD.

But access to the top business brains is only part of the equation. Many women entrepreneurs need additional support to gain the confidence, freedom and opportunities to try out new ways of running and growing their businesses. This is where mentoring can play a hugely influential role.

As a Nigerian, Esisi is no stranger to the concept of mentoring, but in her country it runs along traditional and overtly paternalistic lines. The approach adopted by Goldman Sachs is different, involving a less hierarchical and socially neutral relationship and a considerable degree of e-mentoring. Esisi and her colleagues on the scheme were initially involved in group mentoring by Goldman Sachs executives. The participants feel this still has validity in helping to share collective views and information, but it is not, on reflection, as powerful as individual pairings of mentor and protégé.

The relationship between Pinggera and Esisi grew spontaneously from an initial exchange of e-mails before they actually met. Esisi felt overawed by her mentor's senior management position and began to have doubts about how the scheme could actually work. She recalls:

> She seemed so far removed from my life ... How could I tell this Goldman Sachs MD how badly I had run my business?

Pinggera explains:

> I told her that I had only reached my current position by having mentors. None of us succeeded on our own, we all had help and support.

As for Esisi, she has no doubt what she has gained from 10,000 Women:

> Pinggera drove me forward and made me realise that having a big dream about my own business was nothing to feel guilty about.

CASE STUDY

Veera Johnson

Veera Johnson is chief executive of ProcServe, a UK-based e-procurement enterprise that is helping to change the way that the British government and companies around the world buy from suppliers. Her endeavours led to her being shortlisted for the 2009 Businesswoman of the Year by the Asian Woman of Achievement Awards. Perhaps less well known is her passion for all things pink. The walls in her office are pink, and there's even a pink flash as part of the company branding.

At the start of a recent staff performance appraisal round, Johnson, who is 44, noted that members of her senior team were each sporting something pink on the review day. One was wearing a bold pink shirt, the second a new pink tie and a third, a female colleague, was also dressed in pink. She was both touched and amused by the gesture, which went a long way towards alleviating the anxiety that can accompany such occasions. Though she tactfully declines to say whether the gesture resulted in any pay rises, she says: "It made me realise that I was no longer afraid to be me in front of my colleagues." It was one of those defining moments that she attributes in large part to the effects of the coaching that she received from Aspire, a London-based company that specialises in the development of female executives.

Johnson may have felt she gained greater confidence as a result of her coaching sessions, but it seems that her employer, PA Consulting, with which she set up ProcServe in 2006, had few doubts about her business acumen. She was identified early on in her career in management consultancy as something of a high-flier by her then boss, Michael O'Higgins, formerly head of PA's government and IT consulting group and currently chairman of the UK's Audit Commission.

She made partner level quickly and was sent on an internal leadership development programme that is designed to be rigorous in helping the firm select and develop the right skills in their leaders. She was surprised to learn while on this course that her appointed mentor would be none other than PA's chairman, Jon Moynihan, the man brought in to steer PA back from the brink of bankruptcy in the early 1990s. It was a particularly auspicious start for a young female executive from an ethnic minority background, who was acutely conscious that she had not been to university or college, unlike so many of her colleagues. "They saw something in me that I hadn't been able to see for myself," she recalls.

Many women believe mentoring has been crucial to their career success and Johnson believes that its impact was significant for her too:

> *I think there are people who will advance without the need for mentoring, but I gained a great deal of encouragement and guidance from my mentors.*

She goes on to say:

> *The process of mentoring itself was what really made the difference. The combination of informal mentoring and guided coaching activities forces you to really think hard about what you are good at, what you need to work on, and you can practise making changes and try out different techniques and styles in real live situations.*

The impact of mentoring for her has been significant. Not only does she believe that she has grown in stature and confidence, but she now also applies the same principles to the personal development of many of her ProcServe staff, both junior and senior. The downside to mentoring, she says, is that staying still is not an option. The person being mentored has to be willing to engage and listen to the feedback, and really want to progress and improve.

Those skills have been put to good use. ProcServe, which was established in 2006, has done much to improve the previously poor image of corporate e-procurement, which mushroomed with the dotcom boom but subsided with the bust that followed. One of the features of Johnson's operation, which has made it stand out from many of its rivals, is the sheer user-friendliness of the ProcServe online interface, which makes it more akin to the type of service enjoyed by consumers of eBay or lastminute.com.

ProcServe won a seven-year government contract to deliver a programme called Zanzibar to handle e-procurement in the UK public sector for central government departments and local authorities, which collectively spend an estimated £130 billion with suppliers each year.

Johnson, who has a daughter in her 20s, is aware that career success and the hard work necessary to achieve it can place hard demands on women:

> I think that's why so many companies struggle to retain talented women. As they get more senior they have to balance the expectation that they will continue operating as intensely as when they joined at the more junior ranks.

Management consultancy firms in the UK have come in for their fair share of public criticism in this regard. A survey in 2008 by Experteer, an executive recruitment website, revealed that when it comes to pay in the consulting industry, it most definitely pays to be a man. Men take home average salaries of more than £100,000 while women earn less at under £80,000, the survey showed. This gender gap is likely to remain unless more women like Johnson both attain and retain such senior positions. But has coaching played any part in her career success?

Leadership development at PA includes a degree of personal development but that development must remain rooted in the work context. Johnson was encouraged to seek coaching from Aspire, a London-based coaching firm established by a former HR executive, Samantha Collins. But what did she gain?

> I think the two big things I got out of coaching was an opportunity to become part of a network of female leaders outside my own company who provided me with very useful insights into how they dealt with various workplace situations. Coaching also gave me the courage to be me and not to be afraid of bringing in reference points from outside my own work culture.

Part of that self-expression has been shown by her canny ability to rewrite the rules about how online purchasing takes place by governments and companies. In an interview with the *Financial Times* in 2007 she said:

We tried to relate it back to what experience I would want if I was a public sector employee, so the debate was about usability and not about procurement language.

It is also about having the courage to paint her office pink and to enjoy the gentle ribbing of colleagues as a result.

8 Coaching and mentoring for leadership

And if you are to manage the affairs of the city rightly and well, you must impart virtue to the citizens – which you cannot do unless you possess this virtue yourself.

Alcibiades

Much high-end coaching practice has been focused on the top layer of management where there have been many well-publicised instances of failure. So should coaching share any blame?

The global financial crisis exposed many shocking examples of poor corporate governance and leadership. Alan Greenspan says:

> It's not that humans have become more greedy than they were in generations past, it's that the avenues to express greed have grown so enormously.

Where does this leave everyone else at the top of corporate life? Mostly struggling for survival. Yet one thing that struggling chief executives will not allow themselves to forgo, it appears, is the services of their coach or mentor. Many leading external coaches report that while large-scale coaching development programmes have been cut or cancelled altogether, many chief executives are insistent that they at least get the additional back-up they feel good coaching provides.

"In many cases chief executives are saying they need extra help and support," says Bob Gandossy, head of leadership consulting practice at Hewitt Associates, one of the largest global HR consulting firms, which is based in Lincoln, Illinois, and has annual revenues of more than $3 billion.

While some companies are undoubtedly scaling back on leadership development budgets, some of the best are being even more aggressive on this front in an effort to shore up survival skills. "There's an emphasis on core competencies, particularly the need for agility and a strong top team," says Gandossy, whose firm sponsors the *"Fortune* 100 Best Led Companies" survey, now in its fifth year. Companies are still deploying the services of coaches and mentors, particularly for growth markets in developing economies.

Yet for the past ten years at least there has been no shortage of personal development for those leaders who want it. But some are beginning to argue that the personal development movement, from which much of the coaching industry sprang, is complicit in the leadership failures the global financial crisis brought to light.

Barbara Ehrenreich, author of *Bait and Switch: The (Futile) Pursuit of the American Dream*, says:

> *Many chief executives are delusional. They've been given these crackpot ideas of omnipotence by their coaches and the rest of the self-help industry and it is quite frankly ruining corporate America.*

But not all coaching practice ignores areas of weakness. James McCalman, who heads the Windsor Leadership Trust in the UK, believes a good coach can do much to eradicate such problems:

> *By comparison with traditional management and training, leadership coaching is simply light years ahead because it delivers on an individual one-to-one basis. It is highly beneficial and we know it works.*

McCalman's main beef is with the 35% of business leaders whose egos prevent them from embarking on such development programmes. He says:

> *You would be surprised by the number of very singularly-minded people who think they know all the answers.*

Coaching is fine just as long as it is rooted in reality, according to Gandossy. There is no theoretical substitute for hard work and hands-on experience. The best companies make sure their high potentials gain the right experience through a series of targeted and challenging jobs early on in their career. Gandossy says:

> If companies did more of that they would be able to halve what they currently spend on leadership development and coaching.

This view is shared by two septuagenarian Scottish brothers, William and Kenneth Hooper, respectively a banker and an engineer turned industrial consultants. America was built on the moral legacy of the Puritan fathers, they say in their book *The Puritan Gift*. Old-fashioned virtues of financial responsibility, thrift, craft, hard work and the sublimation of personal interests to the common good were what made America great for 200 years.

The only problem is that the Puritan gift has been squandered. Contrast the above behaviour with the conduct of Joe Cassano, a New Jersey policeman's son and former head of AIG's secretive financial products unit in Mayfair, London, who made a personal fortune of $300m but whose unit's trades helped in large part to scupper the American insurance group.

Business schools bear some responsibility

It is not just rogue traders who are to blame. Much of the guilt also lies with the new breed of professional managers emerging from business schools with an unshakeable belief in their ability to manage corporations with the knowledge they have gleaned from seminars and leadership conferences, says Philip Delves Broughton, author of *What They Teach You At Harvard Business School*, based on his own experience at HBS.

The talk in recent years has been about leadership rather than the real task of management, which is to win orders and customers. Business schools may be actively trying to distance themselves from any blame, but they have been actively complicit in some of the worst excesses that have taken place in corporate America, says Delves Broughton. It was the business schools that insisted on telling their already egotistical young graduates that they were not just MBAs but "future leaders". Among Delves Broughton's list of failures are Stan O'Neal and John Thain, two HBS alumni, who oversaw the demise of Merrill Lynch, once proudly proclaimed as the "Thundering Herd". Andy Hornby, who presided over HBOS's near-collapse, and Rick Wagoner, CEO of General Motors, also attended Harvard Business School.

In a *Financial Times* article in March 2009 Delves Broughton wrote:

> If Waterloo was won, as the Duke of Wellington claimed, "on the playing fields of Eton", then the triumphs and disasters of our recent global economic history had their roots in the class-rooms and cafeterias of Harvard, Wharton, Stanford, INSEAD and other leading schools.

Business schools and companies teach their "leaders" about Marco Polo and Scott of the Antarctic. Some even extolled the virtues of Fred "the shred" Goodwin, the former chief executive of Royal Bank of Scotland, incidentally seen by some at Harvard as the very model of a modern major banker as well as a master of "change management".

Perhaps it is time to get back to the less glamorous basics – the Gradgrind world of spreadsheets, organisational planning and above all sound risk management. What business schools should refrain from doing is to leave their students with the impression that they are anywhere near ready to go out and call themselves "leaders", in any sense of the word.

Perhaps its also time that business schools got back to the more old-fashioned practice of instilling morals into their young charges. More than 20 years ago John Harvey-Jones, who was at the time chief executive of ICI, said: "It horrifies me that ethics is only an optional extra at Harvard Business School."

Shortly before his death in 2004, Sumantra Ghoshal, founding dean of the Indian School of Management in Hyderabad, contentiously castigated the schools in one of his last papers for actively freeing their students from any sense of moral responsibility. The corporate corruption of the early 2000s could be laid squarely at the feet of business schools that taught management simply as a science, he wrote.

Overemphasis on strengths

It is not just business school models that trouble Ehrenreich. They merely reflect, she says, what is going on more widely in the United States. They are in the grip of the same mania that has been created by positive psychology and the self-help movement, which form the target of her new book *Bright-sided: How the Relentless Promotion of Positive Thinking Has Undermined America*. The "science of management" has given way to what she describes as "a wild thrashing around in search of new paradigms to explain an increasingly uncertain world". These include everything from the chaos theory expounded by such gurus as Tom Peters (see page 29) and Anthony Robbins (see page 86) and ancient Native American wisdom.

There may be less fire-walking at leadership conventions these days, and it is doubtful whether the event described in an article, "Religion in the Workplace", in *Business Week*, November 1st 1999, could occur today without shareholders sending round a lynch mob. It involved a session conducted by Richard Whiteley, a Harvard Business School alumnus, who is also described as a "moonlighting urban shaman", with 17 young chief executives in a basement of the luxurious Excelsior Hotel in Rome:

> There in a candlelit room thick with the haze of incense lay the blindfolded captains of industry who breathed deeply as they delved into the "lower world" to the sound of a tribal drum. Whiteley half-whispered above the sea of heaving chests. He then instructed the executives how to retrieve from their inner depths their "power animals", who would guide their companies to 21st century success.

It is not so much talk of "power animals" that frightens Robert Kaiser, a partner at leadership consultancy Kaplan DeVries, based in Greensboro, North Carolina. It is rather what he believes is an overemphasis on strengths-based development, which has been rapidly gaining currency among management teams around the world, but particularly in the United States, where the theory, like so many others, first took root.

The idea of strengths-based development took root at the turn of the millennium with the ideas of Gestalt devotee Marcus Buckingham and his colleague Donald Clifton, joint authors of *Now Discover Your Strengths*. Using research by the Gallup Organisation, where they both worked, their theory essentially attacks most traditional methods of management training and development. They say it is far better to focus and build on people's strengths rather than identify and correct their weaknesses. Working on weaknesses might lift someone's performance by a grade, from D to C, but only by focusing on innate talents or strengths will someone be able to attain an A grade, according to their theory.

Their work has had enormous resonance, not least because it lets managers off the hook for their own shortcomings, says Kaiser, who edited *The Perils of Accentuating the Positive*. It has also formed the basis for much of the strengths-based coaching that has taken root in the past nine years.

Kaiser does not suggest we ignore our talents or strengths; it is just that we are not always capable of recognising them, and that poses real dangers, especially when it comes to running companies. Of course you cannot simply ignore weaknesses, because those flaws are the very ones that can end up derailing your business:

> These fatal flaws are usually evident early in a career but can
> be compensated for by strengths and left to fester.

Moreover, your strengths may not necessarily be the ones your job or organisation requires. Indeed, that is often the case, according to research by the Centre for Creative Leadership. Its survey of the skills and competencies that organisations require in three distinct cultures – the United States, Singapore and India – showed a remarkable similarity of needs: for example, the ability to lead people, strategic planning, managing change and resourcefulness. The survey also showed the same regional similarities in the competencies in which managers were most skilled: respecting individual differences, doing whatever it takes and cultural adaptability.

Thus all three regions showed a gap between what companies needed and the strengths of their managers. By concentrating on their strengths managers would neglect areas of relative weakness, which would damage their respective organisations, the researchers concluded.

Overreliance on strengths is something that also worries Robert Hogan, an authority on personality in the workplace, and Michael Benson, manager of leadership and assessment at Johnson & Johnson. The two big problems in life, they say, are learning to live with yourself and learning to live with others. Strengths-based development is essentially about learning to live with yourself; but leadership is a public act, and unchecked personality flaws and foibles can have disruptive consequences. They are the primary cause of failed leadership and career derailment. Working to address such weaknesses is not such a daft idea, they argue.

This view is endorsed by Catherine Hayes, an expert in organisational development, who has advised a number of global banks based in London and the National Health Service. "Conflict resolution is the number one issue affecting British companies right now," she asserts.

In fast-changing environments a perceived strength might actually turn into a weakness. Scott McNealy, former chief executive of Sun Microsystems, was initially celebrated as a doughty defender of underdogs when he took on Microsoft before the US Congress, but eventually his resolve was generally viewed as bloody-minded obstinacy. This turning of strengths into weakness is also true of global leadership. A style of leadership may work brilliantly in one region of the world but prove disastrous in another.

Strengths-based leadership coaching is a particular threat to American executives, claims Kaiser:

> In the United States there appears to be a cultural halo around everyone's heads. As in Garrison Keillor's fictional home-town, Lake Wobegon, everyone is "above average".

A skilled coach can and often does, however, play a big role in cutting those with big egos down to size, unless of course there is a serious personality disorder involved, such as narcissism. If that is the case, no amount of executive coaching will be able to address it, warns Steve Berglas, a Harvard-trained clinical psychologist, who says that in those circumstances a couch – not a coach – is needed. Giving a narcissist a coach will make everything worse by reinforcing his already overinflated ego with potentially disastrous consequences for his company.

Return to the core agenda

Perhaps a sense of perspective is needed, says Graham Alexander, one of the UK's most experienced executive coaches, who has been working with chief executives of global companies since the early 1980s. Not all those at the top of big corporations are frothing egomaniacs out for their own self-interest. Many are decent people trying desperately hard to do a good job in incredibly difficult circumstances, he says. "I've seen more leadership teams rising to the challenge than falling apart."

There is also a return to the core agenda. A lot of the peripheral stuff is being ditched, says Alexander:

> Everyone is getting down to brass tacks, and any coaching being done right now really has to be directly linked into this. There's less broad vision and more focus on what needs to be done right now, which is no bad thing since the market is going to change very rapidly in the next few years.

This is a view endorsed by Gandossy:

> I think there will be a move to experienced-based coaching very much centred upon business needs. Every executive has blind spots so an independent, trusted outsider who can act as a sounding board does have a valuable role to play.

But he believes there will also be greater discipline as far as coaching is involved.

That discipline will have to come from better, more sustainable business models, says David Brown, chief executive of coaching firm Performance Consultants International:

Before we vilify coaching for any perceived misdemeanours, we need to put things into perspective: coaching, no matter how good or effective, is only a delivery mechanism. It's the business model to which it's attached that really matters. Coaching is meaningless unless it is linked to sustainable business models. If there is no sustainable business leadership, then there can be no meaningful coaching.

Public and private virtue

It is not just about getting good business models right. Senior managers will also have to place greater emphasis on "being" good. Effective leadership, right back to the time of the ancient Greeks, involved a large element of public and private virtue.

Leaders need to be clearer about what they stand for – in other words their values – says leading executive coach David Peterson:

In all the work I've done with people, I'm still surprised at how infrequently people mention the word "integrity" as a value. When I mention this, virtually everyone acknowledges its importance. Often they say, "Well, that's a given", but we need to go further. Where does it rank in their priorities?

People who rank integrity as number one in their priorities will behave very differently from those who rank it only fourth or fifth in their priorities, he says. After all, it is doubtful that Kenneth Lay of Enron, whom many people respected for his community involvement, or Dennis Kozlowski, former CEO of Tyco, or even Bernard Madoff initially set out to deliberately defraud or deceive others.

Peterson, who is vastly experienced in dealing with senior business leaders, acknowledges that digging for deep values is hard work:

When I ask people what motivates them, virtually everyone rattles off four things – money, making a difference, doing the right thing, and running a successful organisation.

While everyone is different, the common theme is that there is no passion in what they are talking about. It is only when Peterson keeps probing that they eventually reveal their deeper values, which for most people is extremely difficult as it is not something they normally do. Money may still feature prominently, but often it is so they can retire to pursue their real passions, or educate their children well so they in turn can lead fulfilling lives.

Extensive research reveals that integrity is crucial to effective leadership. If people sacrifice that virtue, they will eventually lose the ability to lead.

Is coaching to blame?

So if business leadership has floundered, is coaching partly culpable? Not really. There has been excess and froth in the immature coaching industry that in the more sober corporate environment that is already apparent will rapidly disappear. There has been bad coaching and indifferent coaching, as well as effective and occasionally brilliant coaching, but to blame the fledgling industry for the systemic failures of banks and other businesses is not supportable.

Coaching with the bespoke attention that it confers remains a valid process for efficient and speedy dissemination of new business ideas and old-fashioned ethics. As part of an existing array of managerial training interventions, coaching will continue to have an important part to play.

CASE STUDY

Coaching for leadership

The UK's Ministry of Defence (MOD) is increasingly relying on coaching to help develop potential leaders.

Unprecedentedly since the second world war, the MOD has been busy fighting wars on two fronts in Iraq and Afghanistan with what some would describe as a peacetime budget of £35 billion annually. In short, the department has to do more with less in a world where the nature of warfare is changing rapidly. Getting the right people into the MOD's top jobs has never been more of a priority.

The task of filling its most senior posts used to be handled entirely by the MOD's selection board, where the department's most senior civil servants would gather to determine who would obtain the crucial "promotion passport" to its highest ranks. If this did not actually deliver a job, it certainly allowed recipients to apply for job vacancies at senior civil service (SCS) grade.

The only problem was that there were, and still are, only a small number of vacancies available. It is estimated that the MOD makes about 20 senior civil service appointments each year from a potential pool of about 2,500 applicants. Managing expectations in a department where job mobility is traditionally low remains something of a challenge, concedes Jim Butcher, deputy director of talent management at the MOD.

Yet the MOD along with other government departments needs to safeguard its leadership pipeline if it is to raise professional standards and close the skill gaps identified by the Professional Skills for Government initiative across all Whitehall departments.

The application process was reformed in 2004 to make it more fair and open. The selection process is still open to self-nominating candidates and line managers are encouraged to identify those who might not have traditionally put themselves forward for promotion. The interview board has been reinforced by a new set of objective psychometric tests, aimed at assessing personality and verbal and numerical abilities. This is followed by further assessments based on one-to-one exercises, such as dealing with mounting in-trays over a specific period of time.

Just as importantly, the new selection process is designed to pinpoint potential leaders. These are people who are identified as being suitable candidates for the senior civil service who might be ready for promotion within the next 1–5 years.

This middle category became part of a Band B development scheme, which was designed and piloted by Butcher along with his colleague, psychologist Amanda Feggetter, and the rest of his team. Around 25 potential leaders a year join the scheme, which includes an external independent assessment aimed at identifying individual candidates' potential and development requirements, a cognitive behavioural profile, an emotional intelligence questionnaire, role play, a feedback interview and real-life exercises. After the initial test findings have been evaluated, each participant is offered a development plan tailored to their individual requirements.

Traditionally, the MOD has offered its high-fliers a wide range of developmental opportunities including temporary promotions, mentors, seminars, action learning, 360-degree feedback, National School for Government courses and action learning, and so on.

As the development programme was being finalised, the three participating pilot groups were brought together for the first time to discuss the project findings. Surprisingly, when the issue of coaching was raised there was a unanimous show of hands in its support, says Butcher, who, along with Feggetter, is a qualified coach.

But those identified as having high potential wanted external rather than internal coaching. Butcher explains:

> These are all very highly motivated, driven individuals determined to get promotion. They saw external coaching as a safe environment because an outside coach could have no negative influence on their career.

Three coaching companies from the MOD's approved list of suppliers were given contracts to coach the high potentials. In later contracts for the scheme, tenders were sent to some 50 companies.

Individual coaching now forms a major part of the development programme, but it has to be linked to a clear identifiable purpose or goal and fulfil specific development needs. It includes feedback and the involvement of line managers. There are usually eight sessions provided, six of which are normally conducted face to face and two by telephone.

So impressed were some of the candidates with their coaching sessions that they have opted to continue with them, paying for them out of their own pocket. Anecdotally, participants in the scheme said that coaching had made the most significant contribution of all the various management development tools that the programme provided.

After three years 61 individuals had participated in the programme, but seven had withdrawn. It was felt that this was a sufficient number to start evaluating the scheme's overall effectiveness, both quantitatively and qualitatively. Questionnaires were sent to all 54 participants (45 men and 9 women) who had completed the programme to assess how successful it had been in meeting their goals and objectives. These were predominantly to improve strategic thinking, increase their impact and influence, and boost their confidence and self-awareness.

Scheme members were asked to indicate which development activities had been particularly effective in helping them meet their objectives. Executive coaching came out on top, followed by shadowing and communication with those at director level. Coaching was regarded as the most effective tool in terms of helping executives improve their motivation, promotion, job performance and commitment to the MOD. Around 70% of participants responded to the survey.

Further evaluation is under way. There are signs that those who completed the programme may have had more success in job interviews for senior civil service posts than those who did not. Further work also needs to be done to assess how those who went on to obtain senior posts are faring in their jobs. Those who have completed the development programme are also encouraged to consider volunteering to be a MOD mentor, for which they receive specific training.

There was no return on investment calculation. The numbers involved were simply too small, says Butcher. The key measure, he says, remains the ability to fill business critical posts at the right level as and when they arise.

Why does coaching remain so popular with ambitious civil servants? Perhaps it offers the best socially acceptable way of reclaiming some personal, if not elitist, attention in a world increasingly bound by diversity and equality legislation.

Clients' views

Superman don't need no seatbelt.

Muhammad Ali

Does coaching appeal because it is all about personal "me time", or does it really deliver turbocharged performance?

There is a great deal of anecdotal evidence to suggest that when coaching works, it works really well – casting aside often told stories of unfortunate encounters with inadequately trained coaches playing amateur psychotherapist.

Mark Goodridge of ER Consulting, a trained psychologist and HR specialist turned, as he describes, "reluctant coach", says:

> When I do my job well, I help individuals not just to recognise certain character traits or flaws in themselves – grown-ups after all can usually do that for themselves – but more importantly the harder bit, which is recognising how those character traits or flaws might impact on the rest of the company.

What is clear is that coaching is not for the complacent, or the self-satisfied, or for that matter anyone happy with the status quo. "No-one who is content with their life needs coaching," says Vikki Brock.

"It will change your life," says one eager businessman, who forked out the best part of £2,000 to attend a three-day seminar in February 2008 being staged in London's Excel Centre by super-coach Anthony Robbins (see page 86). All this may be true – and predictably on Robbins's website such personal transformation stories abound – but since the same businessman dutifully attends the event most years, it has patently not changed his life to the extent that it does not need a quick refresher from time to time.

Providing inner resilience

Although coaching is much less likely to be offered as a remedial therapy in corporate life, or regarded as a form of punishment for erring or underperforming executives, it is not for the faint-hearted. Coaching can take you to some deeply uncomfortable places, warns Sally Osman, a former senior executive at the British Broadcasting Corporation (BBC). In her case, coaching did not so much stir up a hornet's nest as provide the inner resilience to deal with one not of her own making.

As the BBC's director of communications, she found herself having to help deal with the turbulent aftermath of the Kelly affair – one of the most difficult periods of recent BBC history when both the chairman, Gavyn Davies, and the director general, Greg Dyke, were forced to resign.

Their departures in 2004 followed publication of the findings of Lord Hutton's inquiry into the suicide of David Kelly, a UK weapon's inspector. Kelly had inadvertently found himself at the centre of a political storm after being publicly unmasked as the alleged source for a highly contentious BBC report by journalist Andrew Gilligan. The report struck at the heart of the Blair government by disputing claims that the former Iraqi dictator, Saddam Hussein, had weapons of mass destruction capable of being mobilised within 45 minutes, and thus challenged the legitimacy of the UK's war with Iraq. As a result, the government went on the attack against the publicly funded public service broadcaster.

Osman found herself part of a tight-knit team of senior executives in the strategic hot seat helping to deal with the messy aftermath of the report's publication, which resulted in the dramatic departures of Davies and Dyke. While much of the British media coverage at the time was generally supportive, with some suggesting that the Hutton report had been a "whitewash", it was, nevertheless, a tumultuous period. Osman says:

> I was so close to everything that was unfolding but it sometimes felt very calm in the eye of the storm, which can be a very dangerous place to be.

The coaching she received before and during the crisis was invaluable in that it enabled her to gain an appropriate sense of perspective. She says:

> It is very easy to get too personally involved. Being coached really did help me get through it all. Being able to talk to someone who was dispassionate and only concerned about me was tremendously important.

Ultimately, it helped her to think through how she was going to address specific situations rather than just being carried along by events.

Osman was introduced to coaching shortly after her arrival at the BBC in 1999 and continued to undergo coaching sessions until she left in 2007. Sue Farr, then marketing director of BBC Broadcast, suggested she try it. External coaches had recently been introduced as a development tool for the BBC's most senior executives. It was part of Dyke's motivational drive to make staff more resourceful and creative.

In an organisation traditionally riven by career politics and back-biting, it was often felt things got done at the BBC despite management rather than because of it. Osman explains:

> Greg wanted to make the culture more collaborative, which is why he brought in leading science producer Susan Spindler of Walking with Dinosaurs fame to lead the initiative. If we didn't get a programme maker involved everyone would have been totally cynical.

Although much of the BBC's coaching is now undertaken by an internal coaching team, coaches are still brought in from outside for those at the highest levels of management. Osman was coached by Kate Springford, who she describes as "extraordinary", and who has coached a number of other high-flying female media executives:

> To be honest it took me a while to grasp what coaching was really about, until I clicked that it was about trust, honesty and helping my personal development as a leader.

After an erratic start the sessions continued, sometimes with large gaps in between, but more intensely should the need arise. Osman says:

> The great thing about good coaching is that it sometimes takes you to very uncomfortable places. It can be very challenging. Kate's work with me was often about tackling specific situations such as my role in a particular issue, or my relationship with a particular person, or it could be about something much broader.

Like many women in senior management, Osman had a tendency to assume that if she kept her head down and just got on with the job, all would be well. Coaching introduced a greater sense of vision and control:

> It helped me think about how I was going to address specific situations rather than just being carried along by events. Talking to someone who is completely dispassionate encourages you to think things through more clearly.

There were other tough times at the BBC for her personally. Her big job got even bigger when at one stage she had to take responsibility for TV marketing. The extension of her role, which was arduous enough, was made harder because the BBC was in the process of a major job-cutting programme and her own department was not immune.

It was at times such as those, she recalls, that coaching really helped:

> It helped me work through some very tricky professional issues and understand the importance of not losing sight of yourself and your own values through some very big crises. Being able to rehearse some very difficult conversations and put myself

in someone else's shoes – good coaching techniques – proved invaluable.

It also set her thinking about what else she wanted to achieve in her career:

If you think you have done a job well and done all you can it's not terribly healthy to hang on ... I began to ask the "What if" question as well as what leaving on good terms would mean. Being coached and doing a coaching course myself with Jenny Rogers meant decisions were not made rashly.

Osman left the BBC in 2007 and coaching continues to play a crucial role in her life. She became a coach herself after studying with Jenny Rodgers of Management Futures, a London-based coaching and leadership development consultancy, and practised her skills at the BBC before leaving. She now uses coaching in her role as a consultant to Make Believe, a creative agency, which works with organisations to engage people at brand and organisational levels using the principles and techniques of powerful storytelling. Osman concludes:

Classic coaching skills like listening hard and asking powerful questions work incredibly well when you're trying to reveal a company or brand's authentic story – not the one they think they should be telling you.

Improving communication skills

Better communication with nervous financial investors was one of the reasons one international fund manager cautiously sought coaching. Ramon Garcia Menendez (not his real name) had undergone bouts of enforced leadership coaching while working for a previous employer, a global investment bank based in the United States, with what he describes as "mixed feelings":

Leadership coaching is what institutions use to try and re-energise themselves and is of limited value to entrepreneurs like me.

Menendez heads the sort of financial boutique that in the midst of the global financial crisis might well have been expected to put out a call for coaching to get through what was proving to be an exceptionally difficult market.

His firm, based in London, specialises in high-yield bonds, which at the time of the interview were proving difficult to sell. He says, with studied understatement:

We are facing losses and at the same time have to persuade our limited partners to remain loyal to us, all of which makes forthcoming fund raising challenging.

Unlike leaders in larger financial institutions, Menendez, who nevertheless is managing hundreds of millions of dollars, is relying on a coach for specialist skills training in communications. He is less keen to call in the services of a more holistically inclined leadership coach:

I wanted someone to help me with my presentation delivery, not someone to psychoanalyse me. Communication is obviously vital right now and training to help us do that has already proved invaluable. What we do is highly technical and mathematical. We need to get our story across in a way that is clear and concise.

What began as a week-long training programme with executive coach Hilary Fraser, and has since become regular refreshers, has enabled him to maximise his impact on target audiences:

I think I am much better at making emotional connections with my investors and clients. There is far more structure and clarity in my approach than might have been the case previously.

It has also enabled him to become more attuned to cultural differences in his wide international investor base. He has learned to modify his body language and delivery accordingly.

Communication, however, is only one of the challenges that Menendez faces. Could a coach, skilled in both psychotherapy and psychotherapeutic interventions, help him to navigate the potentially treacherous territory in which he finds himself? Good coaches can help identify the underlying strengths and weaknesses of leaders and help engender an awareness of the choices made in business and in life generally. Menendez, who has had previous leadership coaching, is not convinced. "If I wanted all that stuff, I'd go to a shrink, who is arguably better qualified," he says.

He had previously spent 25 years as an international investment banker, much of it at a senior executive level. He received executive coaching at least once a year which did involve a high degree of psychoanalysis. "It was mandatory," he says. "Everyone at a certain level was forced to do it."

The sessions, which began with feedback from line managers, colleagues and other relevant parties, as well as psychometric profiling, were, he recalls, generally enjoyable. But Menendez says that little of what was done actually "stuck", unlike the more traditional presentation training that he has since pursued:

> There were a lot of questions such as "What was the high point in my career?" as well as "What was the high point in my life?" as well as the reverse of that.

There might be some scope, Menendez concedes, in coaching some of his younger team members, particularly to help them manage their time better. "We endeavour to run a grown-up firm where people respect each other and can manage themselves," he says. But that freedom is not something that the younger members of his team can necessarily readily handle, he concedes:

> They see the five senior partners going off to their own lives, but actually we're working remotely by fax and BlackBerry. They think they should be doing that too, but the fact is, the guys at the top have done their time in the big institutions, we've earned the right to that flexibility, they haven't.

The firm already invests considerable sums in developing its younger fund managers, which would potentially allow for coaching, should it be requested. But so far, team members have invariably opted for language tuition, rather than coaching or other forms of management training.

There might also be a need for those at the top of the bigger institutions to be coached, he concedes:

When institutions take over from entrepreneurs, which will happen to us if we get through the next five years, coaching becomes one of those tools, which people in big companies use to try and re-energise themselves.

Coaching is not a silver bullet for life's ills, warns Menendez. No amount of coaching will make up for market failure or indeed an enterprise whose business model no longer works.

But not all entrepreneurs agree with him. One Jordanian business-man believes that coaching and mentoring have re-energised him and given him access to wider experience and a broader inter-national perspective.

Broadening an international perspective

Mohammad S. Zawaideh, a 31-year-old businessman based in Amman, Jordan, set up OneTEAM Consultants, a management consultancy, in 2005 to provide professional advice, services and training to small and medium-sized enterprises in the Middle East.

The company, which has been growing steadily, has acquired a client base not only in Jordan, but also in Saudi Arabia, Abu Dhabi, Bahrain, Egypt and Lebanon. It is the fruit of several years of hard work, with Zawaideh doing two jobs to earn sufficient money for the launch and having the tough experience of seeing an earlier venture fail.

OneTEAM is one of two start-ups fostered as "incubators" by the Young Entrepreneurs Association of Jordan, which as its title sug-gests is there to encourage a greater spirit of entrepreneurialism in the country. Keen to move on from the incubator stage, Zawaideh has produced an ambitious five-year plan, which should see the company moving into its own offices during 2009, and taking on six full-time staff and up to 20 part-time consultants:

Although we in OneTEAM have succeeded in meeting our busi-ness goals so far, we are still at the beginning.

Like all new businesses, OneTEAM needs to continue to build its client list and revenues. It must also be able to attract bright new talent, whose instincts, like his, upon graduation might be to work for one of the larger international companies. These are issues Zawaideh has discussed at length with his mentor, Anita Weyland, who co-founded her own consultancy firm, Andrum, in the UK in 2006 and is a former HR director of music recording company EMI. She is also a certified coach. Zawaideh says:

> We have established a very good relationship. We stay in touch via Skype and internet. I sent her a sample of the proposals that we sent to our clients, and I asked Anita for her feedback. She has given me a lot of advice. I also asked her to review my five-year business plan and she gave me remarkable feedback.

The relationship was initially fostered a year ago by the Young Entrepreneurs Association, which had linked up with an international mentoring organisation, the Mowgli Foundation. This is the brainchild of Zimbabwean-born Simon Bury, who is now based in Dubai and has spent much of the past three decades founding and running start-up companies in places such as Qatar, Australia and Canada.

Giving local communities, especially those in the developing economies, the tools and know-how to unlock their own potential, rather than aid, is the key to a better, less impoverished world, says Bury. The foundation (www.mowgli.org.uk), which is based in Bristol in the UK, has initially focused its operations on the Middle East, but it plans to extend to other developing regions of the world, such as India, where Bury spent some of his childhood. The idea behind Mowgli was shaped by Bury's encounter in 2005 with management guru C.K. Prahalad, who wrote *The Fortune at the Bottom of the Pyramid* about the 4 billion people on the planet who exist on less than $2 a day.

Zawaideh's introduction to Mowgli was a three-day induction in Amman, where he was interviewed by Mowgli's chief executive, Simon Edwards, a former British army officer, who has extensive experience in the charitable sector. He was also given a detailed induction into what the mentoring relationship would involve on both sides. It was an opportunity to meet several of the mentors participating in the scheme and to gain a sense of who he felt he could work with best:

> *There was a lot of matchmaking taking place. We were also being observed and while the relationships were not forced upon us, I was very happy with the recommendation that I should be mentored by Anita, who is also a consultant.*

OneTEAM was established in 2005, but Zawaideh has been involved in its full-time running for only a little over a year and a half. To be able to fund his venture, he needed to retain his paid employment as a senior executive at the Jordanian Post Company. As director of the operations and services improvement project, he was responsible for co-ordinating the privatisation of the postal services. It was exhausting on both fronts, but the young Jordanian businessman is no stranger to hard work.

Zawaideh grew up in Wadi Rum, a Bedouin community 300km to the south of Amman in the red desert region made famous by Lawrence of Arabia. His father, who had been with the military, quit his job to run his own freight company. Compared with the hardship and poverty suffered by many of the children in his village, Zawaideh's life was relatively affluent, but his family were constantly on the move:

> *I was always changing schools and leaving my friends behind – I absolutely hated it at the time.*

The constant struggle to be successful, which at one stage meant travelling 50km each day to get to a school where he could learn science, which was not taught locally, had an enduring impact on the young man:

> *I grew up realising that nothing would come easily unless you really worked for it, with commitment and passion. I also knew that I wanted to come back and help those who had been less fortunate than me in my community. Maybe there is a boy out there in the desert who has a fantastic dream, but is without the means to make it a reality.*

His father's determination that he should get a good education and his own academic perseverance enabled Zawaideh to attend the

University of Jordan in Amman, from which he graduated as an industrial engineer. At that stage he had little idea that he wanted to run his own company and was happy to accept a graduate post at Nestlé, a Swiss food conglomerate.

It was only after attending an outside training seminar that the desire to set up his own business began to take shape, and it became stronger after he embarked on an entrepreneurship programme run by the UN. "The course involved a degree of coaching, which helped me generate a few business ideas."

However, his first foray into the world of entrepreneurship, acting as an agent for an e-mail services provider, was not a success:

> I was trying to hold down two jobs at the same time and ended up working 18 hours a day seven days a week.

It was untenable, and even though it ended in failure it was good experience.

He began to look at other business projects. The first involved medical tourism. Jordan, a country with a pool of highly trained surgeons and doctors, offers considerable scope for those seeking cheaper operations than can be obtained in the West or in other parts of the Middle East. However, the business plan failed to attract sufficient investment.

Zawaideh's next idea, to launch a firm offering both consultancy and training, offered far better prospects. Using the senior management expertise he gained at the Jordanian Post Company, he was able to gradually build up his fledgling company before finally abandoning his paid employment. Mentoring has been invaluable in helping to guide him through the sometimes lonely task of building his own business. He concludes:

> It is great to have a sounding board and someone to discuss your ideas with. It's also good to have such strong emotional support. With so much misunderstanding in the world today between various civilisations, it is wonderful to have people from Mowgli coming here from the West to help people like me. It is deeply appreciated and I certainly plan to repay that kindness by helping others to succeed in turn.

Cross-border communications

Acquiring a broader international perspective also appealed to John Donovan, a vice-president at Cisco Systems, the world's biggest maker of networking gear. In 2008 he was made head of private-sector business for the UK and Ireland, with an overall responsibility to bring in business from large corporate clients and small and medium-sized enterprises. He also has to run an extended team of sales and marketing and also technical people. It is, he says, a tough environment:

> Everything you read about the economy is true. It is challenging for all our customers and we have to deal with that and help them understand how technology might help them cope better.

In this environment good communication with customers is essential. One of the messages that Donovan will have to convey is that the company is moving beyond the switches and routers that drive traffic over the internet and into computing hardware.

Five years ago Donovan was not so confident about his communication skills. As he rose up Cisco's corporate ladder in the UK, he became aware that his direct and possibly blunt manner, which had served him well in the past, might not be as effective in the wider European environment in which he increasingly found himself as a result of his seniority:

> I became aware that my communication style was typically Anglo-Saxon and might come over to others as abrasive and flippant. I was also aware that I was regarded within the company as a very UK person. I needed to internationalise my approach.

He was at that time a managing director at Cisco, running a division of the company, and as a result of his seniority eligible for external business coaching:

> My then boss instigated coaching for all of his direct reports. It was seen as something for high potentials, rather than remedial or pejorative.

Cisco's HR department worked with an external coaching partner to select four executive coaches for Donovan to interview before deciding which one he felt most comfortable working with. This was followed by a feedback exercise that involved executives with whom he worked:

> I did nominate the list myself, but also made sure I included those whose feedback might possibly be neutral or even negative.

It was an intensive exercise. His coach interviewed all those who had been selected to provide feedback on a one-to-one basis. The results were scrutinised to determine which issues or challenges Donovan wanted to work on; he chose his communication style, particularly where the rest of Europe was involved:

> "I wanted to work on understanding communication styles in different environments and to be able to communicate in the most appropriate way for each of them.

The ensuing coaching took place over a six-month period, with Donovan and his coach meeting on an ad hoc basis either for coffee or to talk on the telephone when time allowed in his busy schedule. Donovan says:

> I had taken a Myers Briggs personality assessment in the past, so had a certain awareness of my personality and behavioural traits, but my coach did a lot more detailed analysis of my style and preferences. I didn't actually find the process uncomfortable. I was receptive to the feedback.

Asking for help

Asking for help, let alone being receptive to anything that could be construed as criticism, is not something that necessarily comes easily to those in the coping professions of medicine and law. But that is exactly what two international lawyers did when confronted respectively with a career crisis and a tough business challenge.

Jo Wilton (not her real name) was facing one of those tough decisions affecting many high-flying female professionals. A mother of two young children, she had applied for promotion at one of

London's leading international law firms and wanted some independent career guidance about how to negotiate terms should the post be offered to her.

She contacted Laurie Adams, a London-based professional mentor with a legal background, who she first came across in an advertisement in a legal publication. Adams had set up Outside Insight, a mentoring and coaching firm. Wilton says:

> I wanted to engage someone privately on my own, without my employer's knowledge or involvement. But it was also crucial to me that I engaged someone who was also a lawyer and understood my own world.

She got more value than she had bargained for. She had stumbled upon someone who not only was empathetic and knowledgeable about her profession, but also had scaled considerable heights in his own career.

Adams, who appeared in *The Lawyer* magazine's Top 100 "Hall of Fame" in December 2007, has spent 25 years as a managing director of, respectively, Lehman Brothers, Citigroup and ABN Amro, working on corporate and legal compliance. He has also been an entrepreneur, having co-led a £50m management buy-out of Siblu Holdings, a French-based caravan site operator; he subsequently helped the company with a £100m refinancing to enable it to fulfil an ambitious expansion plan and remains an investor. In 2008 he was appointed one of the new non-executive directors of Northern Rock, after the UK government bailed out and took control of the Newcastle-based bank, and he chairs its risk committee.

Much of his work has involved building teams of in-house lawyers, introducing him early on to the unexpectedly tough job of managing talent and developing individual team members, which he clearly developed an affinity for. He is also a trained mediator, so the international consultancy Outside Insight, which he set up with business partner Jeremy Thomas, a former partner of Allen & Overy, was an opportunity to apply many of the things he had learned over the course of his career as an in-house corporate lawyer.

Wilton says:

> *What I wasn't expecting was to find such a high level of professional experience. I initially contacted Laurie to seek guidance on how to handle the terms of my anticipated promotion and he was incredibly knowledgeable and helpful.*

But very quickly the bombshell dropped. Wilton did not get the job. She experienced the full gamut of emotions that such setbacks engender: shock, hurt, fury and panic that her failure to gain promotion might actually mean that her career was on the line.

Again the services of her mentor proved invaluable. Wilton says:

> *I was distraught, and while Laurie was very supportive, he was also practical and helped me form a recovery plan.*

One of the real benefits he provided was distance and perspective. He also provided empathy as well as hard-headed insight:

> *He helped me draft difficult emails and was generally very hands on and detailed. But above all he stopped me from flouncing out, which was what I initially wanted to do and which with hindsight would have been a catastrophic mistake.*

Another area where Adams's skills really helped was in handling the so-called work/life balance, something that working mothers in big law firms can find hard to get right. But above all there was a strong element of what the Americans call "tough love".

Wilton had been angry about what she saw as a senior male colleague's decision to exclude her from a particular project over which she felt she had a proprietary interest:

> *I wanted Laurie to side with me and share my indignation over my treatment, but again he made me realise that I was being irrational – ego was getting the better of me. He was right and strangely enough the colleague in question is now a friend and ally.*

She is also confident that her renewed bid for promotion will, this time round, be successful.

Rob Lewis (again not his real name) had worked in a large private practice law firm overseas before accepting a post as head of an in-house team of lawyers for an international financial services institution based in London, which he first had to set up on his own. It was a challenge that he found daunting, since it was not something he had done before. "We needed to set up a world class legal team providing legal services to the business," he says.

A foreigner in London, without much in the way of local knowledge and contacts, and initially feeling culturally at sea, he spotted, like Wilton, an advertisement in a legal magazine for Laurie Adams's professional mentoring services. They met initially for coffee to make sure that they could work together. A meeting was quickly set up that also involved Lewis's chief operating officer. Lewis says:

> It was vital that she was involved at key points throughout the process, especially at the beginning and end. What Laurie did was to put her at her ease immediately by letting her know discreetly that he was never going to interfere with the running of the organisation.

The real benefits of the arrangement were Adams's ability to give pragmatic advice within the constraints of the existing corporate culture. Also, he had extensive experience of similar projects, having set up such teams himself throughout his career. Lewis says:

> What was great for me was the ability to pick up the phone and discuss real non-confidential problems with him. Having someone like him as a sounding board was invaluable. Laurie brought gravitas, sensible recommendations and constructive criticisms about some of my thinking and ideas. I certainly ended up feeling much more confident about what I had to do and my abilities to deliver.

The relationship lasted six months, but Lewis's project will continue for at least ten years, even though, as he says, he is only there to put the building blocks in place.

Could Lewis have achieved his goal on his own, without the help of his professional mentor?

> Yes, I could have got there in the end, but I'm someone who likes playing tennis and I know I play so much better when I've had a bit of coaching.

Raising the game

Raising his game was also one of John Duggan's key objectives. The 61-year-old British-born businessman took a decision in early 2000 to "shake up" Gazeley, a former Wal-Mart in-house property development subsidiary. He and his team turned it into one of the world's largest sustainable warehouse development companies, and one of the tools they used to help them do it was coaching.

Duggan is an enthusiastic proponent of coaching, having experienced at first hand many of its benefits. He has made it his business to uncover coaching's various psychological underpinnings and, dauntingly, some of the more esoteric developments taking place in the related field of neuroscience.

He rattles off the names of several scientists and academics associated with this field who may be important but are not yet mainstream. He is keen to debate whether the behaviourists have got things right – he is not so sure. Neuroscience seems to hold great promise:

> Perhaps it will allow people to get better or improve performance more efficiently and humanely than some of the psychotherapeutic interventions currently on offer.

It would be a mistake, however, to assume that Duggan, having made his pile at Gazeley, has embarked on some sort of new-age love-in. He may be a vociferous champion of "green" business and endlessly fascinated by psychology, but "eco" in his book – he is an accountant by training – stands as much for "economical" as it does for "ecological":

> The trouble with a lot of people that go into coaching is that they come from new-age backgrounds and lose their brains in the process. I don't have a closed mind and am happy to look at different paradigms, but I believe that the process has to be grounded in reality.

His pursuit of these ideas and coaching coincided and indeed played a key part, he says, in helping him transform Gazeley. The company had been the in-house property arm of ASDA, a UK supermarket chain, which along with Gazeley was sold to Wal-Mart in 1999.

Under Duggan's watch Gazeley was transformed into an international property company that developed sustainable warehousing in Europe, as well as in China, Mexico and India. Over the nine-year year period of Wal-Mart's ownership, Duggan, with a team of just 75 employees, tripled Gazeley's profits to about $50m a year. The company moved from being a business that was essentially high-volume, low-value to being one of those agile, fast-moving 21st-century companies so beloved of business academics. As a result it became more complex and high-risk, but also much more high-value and attractive to outside buyers.

Gazeley was sold in June 2008 to Dubai World for a sum speculated to be in the region of $800m. It was at this point that Duggan, who had been Gazeley's chief executive and then its chairman, left the company.

Duggan's nine-year transformation of Gazeley began with a simple desire:

> I wanted to take my company and shake it up, and I looked to coaching as one of the tools that I could use to do that. I wanted to release a lot of energy and potential.

But that first involved exploring his own underlying motivations:

> I needed to get a better understanding of why we always act or behave in certain ways and keep repeating those patterns, whether good or bad. I wanted to become more self-aware so that I could make better choices and be a better leader of the business.

He was also conscious of the dramatic changes taking place in the world around him. It was both shrinking and changing, and the pace of those changes was changing the tectonic plates of the western culture in which he found himself:

> I became convinced that the patterns of behaviour that we learn from our families and even from the very best educations no longer necessarily provide us with the best preparation.

He also made a decision that if he remained at Gazeley, he would change it from a UK-based operation to the one that it has grown into today, which operates in ten countries.

As part of his quest to release the energy and potential within Gazeley's warehousing business, one that many think of as dull rather than involving cutting-edge environmental technology, Duggan began to consider coaching. He took the advice of and eventually hired an executive coach, recommended to him by fellow businessman John Harrison, one of the co-founders of Marylebone Warwick Balfour (MWB), a property group which had found developmental coaching useful. The coach, the late Leslie Lewis, had worked with MWB and Vodafone and had coached many senior executives. He promised that coaching would enable Duggan and his team to understand their underlying strengths and weaknesses as well as the impact they made.

The process kicked off with an intensive series of interviews by the coach or HR department with close working colleagues of the person going to be coached concerning his strengths and weaknesses. Duggan was sanguine about the ensuing feedback, which revealed that while he possessed vision and the ability to inspire and lead his team, he also had potential weaknesses when it came to some of the finer points of organisational processes. The analysis enabled him to build on his strengths, but also, importantly, to address any deficiencies, by making sure he had the people that would make his team the strongest possible. He recalls:

> I considered the initial coaching experience a good investment, but it was only the beginning.

Already an avid reader of psychology, philosophy and new science, Duggan personally followed up with more coaching, this time using several people: Sir John Whitmore (see page 71), one of coaching's early pioneers and founder of Performance Consultants International; Hetty Einzig, a senior consultant at Performance Consultants International; and independent consultants Helen-Jane Nelson and Lynda Cant. He also embarked on a bout of psychotherapy and attended classes on Buddhist psychology.

What did his colleagues at Gazeley, all of whom were involved in

transformational coaching aimed at heightening their self-awareness, make of the process? Duggan says, candidly:

> *I think some of my people thought at the time that it was a load
> of rubbish, but later they conceded that they had learned a lot.*

And how did those running ASDA react to the changes under way?
ASDA may be known for the efficient selling of cut-price supermarket goods, but not necessarily coaching and psychotherapeutic
interventions.

You have to understand, says Duggan, that many of the big UK
retailers, including Tesco, J. Sainsbury, Kingfisher and Dixons, had
set up their own in-house property development operations, just
as ASDA had done in the late 1980s, but none had grown into successful standalone businesses in the way that Gazeley had done:

> *Because the company was profitable we had a high degree of
> credibility and we had a relatively free hand.*

Archie Norman, who ran ASDA from 1996 to 1999, had been supportive of Gazeley and so too had successive ASDA chief executives who had personally supported Gazeley's earlier growth
strategy. But added impetus came with Wal-Mart ownership in
1999. Wal-Mart's chief executive, Lee Scott, and chairman, Rob
Walton, had clearly seen the company's potential. "They gave us
their full support," says Duggan.

That support crucially enabled Gazeley to press on with its plans
for international expansion in what is a highly competitive market.
The process began with regular brainstorming sessions and the use
of low-tech blackboards. Duggan recalls:

> *One of the things I tried to do was to help our people realise the
> impact that they had on other people. I wanted them to think
> about how they could become more effective as leaders. It was
> essential to get each and every one involved.*

Coaching was also part of the transformation process. Without it
Duggan doubts that the outcome would have been so successful:

> *We certainly made mistakes along the way and didn't always
> behave as well as we could have, but we were at the end of the*

day accountable. We would put our hands up and go back and find a better way of doing things.

Coaching helped Duggan align Gazeley's people, business activities and processes around the company's shared vision, which was to "be a global provider of logistics space" and to "inspire business to work with nature to create a sustainable world".

One of the ways in which the company worked to create a more sustainable world was to ensure that all future developments were built to high environmental standards, a move that added a small percentage to building costs. But this was more than offset by the lower running costs enjoyed by operators, particularly the premium customers that Gazeley was able to attract because of its strong eco-credentials. These included DHL, Procter & Gamble and John Lewis, a British retailer. Dino Rocos, distribution director at John Lewis, says:

The thing that drew us to Gazeley was that from our very first meeting they had a green agenda.

But warehouse operators apparently pay no more for the 11 energy and water-saving features fitted as standard than they would for a more traditional warehouse with four walls and tin roof. These include solar thermal heating, rainwater collection, energy-efficient lighting, recyclable floor coverings and timber from sustainable sources.

Wal-Mart launched its own global initiative on climate change in 2005, two years after Gazeley opened its first facility based upon sustainable principles.

Duggan's legacy continues. By 2010 Gazeley has pledged to make a 35% overall global reduction in its carbon emissions. It has also committed to reuse or recycle 50% of all construction waste. So too does his interest in sustainable business. He is currently chairman of Spazio Investment, an Italian property investment fund listed on the UK's AIM (alternative investment market). He sits on the advisory board of the Doughty Centre for Corporate Responsibility at Cranfield University in the UK, and was until recently a member of the board of the China-US Centre for Sustainable Development and a member of the US advisory council for the Prince of Wales's Business and the Environment Programme.

The knowledge gained at Gazeley can be useful elsewhere, he says, particularly in these unprecedented and challenging financial trading environments:

> *The time is right. Business has to be more socially responsible, because quite frankly the current generation is going to be very damning of us if we duck this challenge.*

Coaching remains one of the perks for the most senior in corporate life, but arguably could be even more effective further down the hierarchical chain. Duggan remains convinced that the success of Gazeley was built not only on his own endeavours, but also on those of his team, all of whom received coaching as part of the planned company transformation.

The future

> How far you go in life depends on your being
> tender with the young, compassionate with the
> aged, sympathetic with the striving and tolerant
> of the weak and strong. Because someday in
> your life you will have been all of these.
>
> George Washington Carver

Coaching lacks a proper cross-cultural identity and is still widely regarded as a finishing school for senior executives. This may change as coaching and the related activity of mentoring extend more widely beyond the world of business, other organisations and government into such areas as medicine and even childhood. The emerging field of neuroscience may offer new insights, but whether such developments are benign is a matter of debate.

What is coaching actually for? We have a broad idea of what coaching does, as discussed in earlier chapters, but what purpose does it ultimately serve? We know that good coaching – or mentoring – is supposed to enhance individual or group performance. But there is compelling anecdotal evidence to suggest that its emergence as a new "profession" is in large part a response to something important that is missing from our lives. We also have a feeling that unless the activity is tied to a sustainable business or organisational model it will somehow fail to deliver its goals. There is also a sense that coaching and mentoring in a secular world should promote virtue, rather than sustain the unsustainable or immoral.

Coaching is an ambitious discipline that has assumed a world view, but that view is largely American despite the elements of Eastern religion or mysticism that coaching has absorbed. It has flourished in other western-based cultures such as the UK and Australia but cannot truly be described as "cross-cultural".

Belgium-born coach Philippe Rosinski, author of *Coaching Across Cultures*, recalls a meeting with a Japanese woman who told him that many of her fellow citizens had come to accept American models of management at the expense of older Japanese traditions. He says:

> Universalism, individualism and directness – typical US cultural orientations – may not feel right to the Japanese but given the success and dominance of the US, the Japanese accept that the American way must be right.

Rosinski is referring to cultural differences not just between nations, but also between generations and even companies. Different generations inevitably look at life and work, and live their lives, differently from each other. And the world of business is full of companies that have embraced different organisational cultures, values and aims, and ways of working.

Instead of talking about a clash of cultures, or overcoming what C.K. Prahalad referred to as the "imperialist mindset", coaching should be doing more to bridge the gap that exists not only between people from different cultures, but also between those from different organisations and backgrounds.

Coaching can help draw out the best from various disciplines and cultures. For example, Rosinski talks about the Japanese prevailing cultural propensity for harmony with the environment in contrast to the American desire for control over the environment. These two propensities, he argues, need not be mutually exclusive. Japanese managers can foster harmonious relationships that underpin team cohesion, while at the same time benefiting from the more direct style of communications found in the United States, where managers feel the need to be more proactive about forging the future.

One feature of coaching is the cultural mismatch it tends to bring to a business environment. With few exceptions, coaches are ferociously co-operative rather than ferociously competitive. This may strike a discordant note in the intensely competitive world of global business, but it may prove highly effective in forging new, collaborative business models more in tune with a world of bewildering complexity and change.

Two areas in which coaching could make an increasingly positive difference in future are in health care and with children, notably troubled children.

Health care

Being more in tune with clients – or rather patients – is something that many doctors would greatly benefit from. Siraj Bechich, a physician and co-ordinator of King Juan Carlos's personal medical team, believes coaching is the key not only to better patient care in Spain and elsewhere, but also to preventing problems of burnout in doctors. He says:

> The overwhelming majority of people die from only two diseases – atherosclerosis and cancer – and both are largely preventable.

In other words, lifestyle and temperament – bad diet, drinking too much, smoking too much, being too much of a couch potato and being downright gloomy – can unleash the three evils of the health apocalypse: heart disease, stroke and cancer (though these may also have genetic origins).

Bechich, a pioneer in clinical preventive medicine at the privately run International Centre of Advanced Medicine (CIMA) in Barcelona, knows a thing or two about bodily failure, or rather how to avoid it. He is also a qualified coach, who believes that his skills in this area have added an invaluable new dimension to his job as a clinician. Indeed, he believes coaching is the missing link in the failure of many New Year resolutions. In other words, simply telling others what they must do or desist from rarely produces desired results, especially in the field of medicine. Research suggests that a staggering number of people lie to their doctors about their true level of alcohol consumption, as well as other aspects of their lifestyle. Self-help slimming manuals regularly top the best-seller lists, yet signs of failure – certainly in the affluent West – are everywhere as populations grow ever more obese. Bechich says:

> Coaching means that I tend to have a very different approach from more traditional colleagues. It's about treating patients as equals and not ordering them to do this or that, but working with them to identify and achieve their own health goals; it is about raising their self-awareness and self-responsibility for their own health.

Bechich, who also has expertise in treating infectious and auto-immune diseases, has looked outside the confines of his own profession to acquire new skills to enhance his work as a doctor. He has a degree in Integrated Health Services management from ESADE, a leading business school based in Barcelona.

His move into coaching was more accidental, a fortuitous internet discovery made while researching something else. By qualifying as a coach, he has been able to formalise much of what he did instinctively as a caring doctor. Bechich, who is accredited by the International Coach Federation and is a senior adviser for coaching and consulting firm Performance Consultants International, says:

> I think that I was always an instinctive coach. I felt very comfortable with its concepts of listening, questioning, communicating, challenging, creating awareness, establishing and working towards goals and above all of building trust and intimacy.

Coaching has also been deployed in the running of the Spanish king's medical team, where Bechich plays a pivotal role as its co-ordinator. More than 50 doctors, nurses and health technicians are involved in the intensive annual day of tests involving the king. Bechich says:

> To care for the constitutional head of state is a great honour and responsibility. I have used my coaching skills and I like to think that they have helped put together a highly effective team of people. It's all about listening, challenging, empowering. Above all it is about establishing absolute trust, something that is vital to the dynamics of a team.

Aside from his day-to-day duties, he has been coaching a group of three women, two of whom have had cancer, as part of an ambitious project to create a series of drop-in centres for cancer patients and their families, similar to the Maggie's Cancer Caring Centres established in the UK by the late Maggie Jencks. The Spanish project, which aims to establish its first centre in Barcelona, will be based on the same concepts of architecturally arresting buildings set amid beautiful landscaped gardens. They too will adjoin existing oncology clinics or hospitals, but will be run independently of them.

The idea is that this sanctuary will complement the work of oncologists and do what hospitals often cannot, which is to take time to inform, listen and support cancer sufferers and their families, who need comfort, space and above all hope in order to come to terms with what has happened to them. Bechich explains:

> It all began when my patient, a Scotswoman living in Barcelona, returned to her native country after diagnosis and visited a Maggie's Centre. She was inspired by what she found there so that on her return to Spain, where there is nothing comparable, she set out to replicate it over here. I feel certain that she and her two colleagues will succeed in their venture.

A cancer diagnosis, he explains, can be utterly overwhelming, if not devastating. But it can also be empowering. Those who have experienced it often discover an appetite for living that makes them fully focused on more important things such as love, kindness, joy and peace. Says Bechich:

> Team coaching builds on this experience and has contributed to the success of the Barcelona project.

But not all his colleagues in the medical establishment share his views. The autocratic approach – even the term "patient" is a passive one – still predominates, and not just in Spain. Healthcare systems may do a good job caring for and treating millions of patients, but they are run with what many might describe as an outdated command and control mentality. "It's about patients doing what they're told rather than equality and partnership," says Bechich.

That approach, combined with heavy workloads and the high stress levels involved in making life and death decisions, goes some way towards explaining why so many doctors suffer from professional burnout and stress. Coaching, Bechich believes, can play an invaluable role in helping to prevent such disastrous consequences for both the doctor involved and the patients who may be harmed by such hidden problems.

Bechich is actively involved in coaching initiatives aimed specifically at medics suffering from high stress and burnout in the United States. He says:

> In a very non-judgmental way, coaching helps create self-awareness in an individual, which is the first step towards wanting to get better. The essence of being a physician is "the calling" and one's own purpose in life. Coaching facilitates the connection to one's own purpose, from that place doctors can increase their performance as well as prevent spiritual failure.

The medical profession has been slow to adopt coaching initiatives but is showing some signs of receptivity. Barcelona's Official College of Physicians has already delivered its first training session in medical coaching. There are further plans among coach-doctor pioneers, such as Bechich, to train medical students in coaching skills at the Central University of Barcelona. It will be this upcoming generation of doctors who will change medicine for the better, claims Bechich.

Children

The upcoming generation is something that also preoccupies Christine Miller, a former management consultant turned business coach and mentor. She decided to focus her skills on helping children after being profoundly affected by the suicide of her daughter's 17-year-old school friend. The girl, who came from a loving middle-class home and attended a private school, had been anxious about her schoolwork, about her appearance and about whether she was popular with her peers – normal teenage concerns that had somehow spiralled out of control.

"It had such a profound effect on the family, the school and the local community," she recalls. It was also a personal clarion call to Miller, who lives in London and who had used coaching techniques in the upbringing of her own children, to refocus much of her work on helping troubled youngsters. It was a difficult personal decision since it indirectly reconnected her to an earlier career as a schoolteacher, which she believed had ended in personal failure.

She had taught at a school where her largely middle-class charges were both intelligent and motivated and where she had thrived. It was only when she moved to a more challenging post teaching 15-year-old girls from poor families in an inner-city school that things began to change for the worse. Miller says:

> These girls were one step away, in many cases, from being excluded by the authorities. It was my job to teach them French and while I tried very hard to make it as exciting a subject for them as I could, they were contemptuous. They just couldn't see the relevancy of it to their own lives. Their expectations were so low.

She left feeling that she had failed her pupils. She then embarked upon a successful career in research and consultancy where she worked in senior posts at a number of big companies, including Fiat, before eventually becoming involved in training large groups of people:

> I found that supporting people to be at their best was my forte, and also what I really love doing.

The death of her daughter's friend prompted her to confront her old nemesis – working with troubled teenagers – but this time she was armed with her coach training expertise, which had also given her a grounding in therapy and psychology. There has been no shortage of work. Almost 1.3m children in England have "special needs", representing 16% of children across all schools, according to government statistics in 2007.

Increase in emotional disorder

It is a worldwide phenomenon, explains Martin Seligman (see page 19), professor of psychology at the University of Pennsylvania and one of the principal architects of the "positive psychology" movement. Depression was relatively rare until the 1960s, and usually experienced by middle-aged women. But in the past 30 years it has become much more prevalent, affecting much younger people.

Seligman writes in his book *The Optimistic Child*:

> *Depression has become the common cold of mental illness and it takes its first victims in junior high school – if not before.*

He cites several studies carried out in the United States. The first of these, known as the ECA study, published in 1993 and involving 18,571 people, surprised statisticians. Those born around 1925 generally showed little sign of depression and only 4% had experienced severe depression by the time they reached middle age. Of those born before the first world war, only 1% had suffered from depression by the time they reached old age. But things began to change when the self-centred feel-good era got under way, with 7% of those born around 1955 suffering from severe depression by the time they reached their early 20s.

A second American study cited by Seligman looked at 2,289 close relatives of 523 people who had been in hospital with severe depression and again the findings were, he says, "astonishing". They reveal a dramatic increase in rates of depression over the course of the 20th century. More than 60% of women born in the early 1950s had, according to the study, been severely depressed, compared with only 3% of women born around 1910. A similar pattern also emerged for males.

Our grandmothers' generation might have dismissed much of what is currently labelled depression as "just life", but that does not explain the increasing numbers of individuals who have cried every day for a fortnight, lost rapid weight over a short period of time without dieting, or tried to kill themselves. Disturbingly, it is a trend that shows little sign of abating. A study of 3,000 children aged 12–14 in the south-eastern United States suggested that a staggering 9% suffered from depression.

What are the causes?

So what or who is to blame for this increase in emotional disorder? Seligman points the finger at baby-boomer parents, whose self-preoccupation has changed society from one valuing achievement to a feel-good one. The right to self-esteem has even become enshrined in Californian law. Poor self-esteem is supposedly behind academic failure, drug use, teenage pregnancy and welfare dependency, and yet all those ills are on the rise.

It is nonsense to tell children they have done well when they have not. You are in effect lying as well as creating false expectations, which when they are not met will set up children for disillusionment and possibly depression, says Seligman, who urges parents instead to teach their offspring resilience and optimism to handle life's slings and arrows:

> The goal [of achievement] was then overtaken by the twin goals of happiness and high self-esteem. This fundamental change consists of two trends. One is toward more individual satisfaction and more individual freedom: consumerism, recreational drugs, day care, psychotherapy, sexual satisfaction, grade inflation. The other is the slide away from individual investment in endeavours larger than the self: God, nation, family, duty. Some of the manifestations reflect what is most valuable about our culture, but others may be at the heart of the epidemic of depression.

The negative aspects of that culture change has created extensive damage, particularly to children, something that Gail Manza, executive director of the National Mentoring Partnership (NMP) in America, is acutely conscious of. Much of the NMP's work centres on socially deprived children from chaotic backgrounds, where it is not uncommon for one or more parent to have a history of drug or alcohol abuse, or to be in prison. Yet what these socially deprived young people need, she says, is not mollycoddling or even necessarily cash handouts, but the means of getting access to the right resources to enable them to get some degree of control over their lives.

Ean Garrett, who is now at law school and a mentor himself, is one of the NMP's stars. He grew up in the direst of circumstances in America's mid-west. His mother was in prison for killing his father and as a boy he was shunted from one relative to another until mentors became involved in his life. Garrett recalls:

> From the start I was expected to lose. Everything I have right now is mostly because I defied what the world concluded about me before I could even speak a word in my defence. And my defence is that I am just as capable as any person to do great things. Like you, I think about all the things this world could achieve if only every child was given the right tools. Mentoring is the right tool.

He has already amply demonstrated that by graduating from Howard University in Washington and then winning a scholarship to law school in Nebraska.

Before the NMP was launched in 1990, Geoff Boisi and Ray Chambers, the two philanthropists who founded the organisation, set out to canvass opinion among the youth of America by personally interviewing them at boys' and girls' clubs in several American states. They wanted to find out what they felt was missing from their lives and how it could be addressed.

Two universal themes emerged from their endeavours. The children said they wanted to be part of the "American Dream" but felt they had been excluded. They also wanted more adult contact in their lives, not less. Boisi and Chambers concluded that a lack of caring adult role models to guide and support young people was at the heart of the problem. Mentoring was believed to be the most effective way of meeting those twin needs.

But it is not just the deprived that need help. Privileged youngsters may be suffering similar pressures, albeit of a different nature. Unlike the underprivileged, they may be experiencing a surfeit of parental involvement to the extent that it stunts their development and ability to grow up. This tendency has been exacerbated by the arrival of the mobile phone – what some have dubbed the world's longest umbilical cord. There is even a new Google program called Latitude that allows overprotective parents to track their children's every movement.

The rising cost of private education and university fees has reinforced what is known as "helicopter parenting" – parents who just cannot let go of their children. Some even insist on accompanying their offspring to university careers fairs, quizzing prospective employers and generally interfering in every aspect of their children's lives. All this bodes badly for society, warns Frank Furedi, professor of sociology at Kent University in the UK. It will lead to its "infantilisation".

American clinical psychologist Madeline Levine agrees:

> Kids are unbearably pressured not just to be good, but to be great; not just to be good at something, [but] to be good at everything.

Happiness classes

Those pressures are something that Anthony Seldon, headmaster of Wellington College in the UK, is acutely aware of and why shortly after his arrival at the school he implemented happiness classes for pupils aged between 14 and 16.

The UK came bottom in a 2007 UNICEF survey of life satisfaction among children in 21 most developed economies, which Seligman, on a visit to Wellington College in 2008 to attend a conference on positive psychology, slated as "a national disgrace". Seldon, a well-known political biographer and no intellectual slouch, believes that what he describes as "the toxic obsession" with endless exams and tests is partly to blame. It has obscured something far more important – namely the overwhelmingly important task of producing happy, well-adjusted young adults.

Seldon, who believes that happiness classes should be more widely available and not just for his wealthy young charges, says:

> Celebrity, money and possessions are often the touchstones for teenagers and yet these are not where happiness lies.

The classes, which have been running for three years, have proved popular with both parents and pupils. Even teachers, some of whom were initially sceptical, believing that the scheme might be a PR stunt aimed at overcoming bad publicity about instances of bullying among pupils, are now positive about the benefits.

The classes were put together with the involvement of Nick Baylis, a psychologist and co-director of the Well-being Institute at Cambridge University established in 2006, and are run by Ian Morris and the rest of the school's religious education staff. They involve meditation as well as discussions about happy and successful lives and overcoming adversity, not only through dealing with situations arising in school, such as one pupil being unpleasant to another, but also through exploration of famous inspirational lives. The example of Lance Armstrong, who overcame cancer to win the Tour de France several times, is a popular topic.

Instilling resilience

Christine Miller also believes that instilling resilience into her young clients is crucial to their well-being. She has a master's degree in Counselling Practice and is qualified to Master Practitioner level in neuro-linguistic programming (NLP), hypnosis and a methodology called time line therapy designed to release negative emotions. Miller says:

> I coach them in accelerated learning techniques, learning how to learn, coupled with building rapport and learning to read other people's body language through non-verbal intelligence and thereby assess the response they are getting.

She believes that family breakdown and the decline of extended families are part of the reason she has found a receptive market for her work:

> There are fewer elders for children to go to for help and guidance. At one time, it used to be that if you had a disagreement with your mother or father, you could probably find a relative – an aunt, uncle or grandparent – to go and talk things over with, and get the benefit of some wise, impartial advice, or at least step out of the situation to gain perspective, but these days we're more spread out, much busier and children can end up being very isolated with their problems.

Her work centres on children and young people aged between seven and 18 and usually involves 10–12 sessions. The cost is kept to the equivalent of other extracurricular activities such as music lessons. Miller also undertakes pro bono work for problem children whose parents cannot afford such fees:

> I tend to get sent the kids who are in trouble – about to be excluded from school, having problems at home – and I'm often something of a last stop before they get referred to the Education Psychology Service.

Often her young clients have behavioural problems and have been violent and aggressive. Others suffer from sadness and depression. They may have been bullied or are the perpetrators of bullying, or are underachieving academically. But not everyone can be helped:

> I do choose my clients – I do an assessment or a trial session from which I quickly determine if someone is coachable – and I have very firm boundaries in place.

She tries to involve the whole family, wherever possible, because they can play a determining role in a child's behaviour. Often a child is merely conforming to the family stereotype that has been set, such as the "naughty child", "the difficult one" and the "not-too-bright one". Uncovering those unseen influences is crucial if the child is to change, she explains.

One mother brought her 17-year-old daughter to see Miller and dominated the conversation, hardly allowing her daughter to speak:

> She simply criticised and poured out a catalogue of the ills that she saw in her child. When I got to spend time with the girl, she told me that her mum wouldn't let her do anything that 17-year-old girls usually do – wear make-up, go shopping, go to discos (she'd been prevented from going to the school dance then been criticised for not having friends). Films and boyfriends were totally taboo as well.

What Miller did in handling this difficult situation, which in essence involved an extremely dominant and intolerant father, was to teach the daughter rapport-building and negotiation skills. "I also helped her find some inner resources." She also worked on the mother to impress upon her husband how intelligent, strong and resourceful the daughter really was.

Confidentiality is a delicate issue with children – some parents expect full feedback, which can inhibit what a child will share in the sessions. So Miller operates a policy of something called "informed forced consent", which means that everything remains confidential unless there is a perceived danger to the child. She says:

> Obviously, if there were to be concerns about safety then the ethical guidelines by which I am bound [those of the British Association for Counselling and Psychotherapy (BACP)] would come into play and appropriate action would be taken. My job is essentially to help these young people find peace and happiness and a stimulus to succeed in their lives, whatever the definition of a successful outcome may be. In the extreme cases, I help them to pause, to stop and think before they break that window, smash the chair, hit someone or even draw that knife.

Often her clients are sent by either their parents or their teachers and do not want to be there:

> They're what I call hostages – and winning their confidence and trust is of key importance, so whatever we do has to be relevant and engaging.

It is important to find out what they want – what they believe would make their lives better – not just what the school or the parents think should be happening:

> In the beginning I help them find something they're good at – and there always is something, some memory of a moment they felt really good about – then we build on that as a resource.

There are explorations and visualisations to build a safe space and a resourceful state of mind. And her young charges are taught simple self-management techniques based on martial arts and sports, accelerated learning methods, such as learning to count to ten in Japanese in five minutes, and practical skills like mind-mapping, which help to integrate the hemispheres of the brain. All this is designed to help build their confidence and sense of self. It is a delicate process working with younger children; the balance of power is crucially important since they possess little in the way of autonomy. Miller says:

> It's not helpful to anyone if they resent being with me, so I

always include an element of choice and am flexible, making space for them to suggest what they might want to do.

Storytelling plays an important role, as does creating metaphors to express what it feels like when they are in different states of mind. If they create their story in their own words, they are not going to argue with or resist their own creations, and this will often lead to big breakthroughs and self-discovery. The experience must be as natural and enjoyable as possible, explains Miller:

Laughter tends to be a common factor, we play music, do drawings, and we use the computer for games and to watch ways of handling different behaviour scenarios.

There are homework tasks, but not too many or too onerous. It is part of building a habit of accountability, she says:

The main factor is to offer them what Carl Rogers described as "unconditional positive regard", completely non-judgmental, to be a mirror so they can see themselves as worthwhile, lovable and loved, and thus take personal responsibility.

Any such engagement involves a degree of discussion over outcomes: what is clearly achievable and what is unrealistic and how such outcomes might be recognised by Miller and her clients. But the best outcomes involve getting telephone calls, weeks, months, or even years after the coaching experience, informing her of the success of past clients, whether that means staying off drugs, passing exams or finding the inner resilience to deal with bullying.

Feedback comes from parents, from teachers and most importantly from the children themselves. If previous academic failure is involved, improved school reports are usually a good benchmark that the intervention is working. Miller says:

Sometimes the mere fact that the child is turning up at school or that they haven't been excluded since we began working together is a good indicator of success.

So too are reports of fewer arguments between child and parents.

But success is on a limited scale in a society where so many children are beset by emotional and behavioural difficulties. "I would like to spread my work much further," says Miller, who would like to share her skills with schools.

Schools cannot be expected to do everything, or to compensate for neglectful or domineering parents. However, coaching and resilience training show promising signs of doing something to help children under pressure who, for whatever reason, have been unable to find the right level of support from family or friends.

Conclusion

Coaching generally continues to offer promise. Many claims have been made about its efficacy in helping people change in positive, if not life-transforming ways. But what we still do not know for sure is how many of those changes are lasting.

Some people doubt its overall efficacy as they might with, say, psychotherapy or homeopathy, while others, especially those who have been coached, take a more (even wholly) positive view of coaching. But there is a suspicion held by many people that human beings invariably revert to type, no matter how good the coaching, and that our brains are simply too hard-wired from an early age by our genetics and life experiences to alter to any radical degree.

Many coaches are awaiting new developments in the burgeoning field of neuroscience, which they instinctively believe will somehow support pet theories about what they actually do, most of which have still to be subjected to rigorous scientific evaluation.

As American writer Tom Wolfe said in a 1996 essay "Sorry But Your Soul Just Died", current brain imaging devices used for medical diagnosis may eventually be replaced by far more sophisticated models that can not only determine what is likely to be genetically wrong with us, but also cast light upon the great universal questions such as "self", "mind", "soul" and "free will".

We may be on the threshold of great advances, finding not only cures for desperate afflictions such as Parkinson's disease, Alzheimer's and schizophrenia in the coming years, but also things that shed light on why people think and behave in certain ways.

Among those who eagerly await such developments is David Rock, an Australian-born executive coach, who has developed a neuro-leadership programme in an attempt to incorporate some of the existing findings from neuroscience into his coaching practice:

> Neuroleadership is about helping leaders understand how their own and their people's minds and brains actually work, replacing our current guesswork. Humans have a long history of incorrect assumptions about the world.

Unravelling the secrets of the human brain may be the new frontier as far as medicine, or even coaching, is concerned. But it is a voyage of discovery that is unlikely to be completed soon, despite some of the more enthusiastic expectations. This leaves coaching, for the time being at least, dependent on experience, instinct, ancient wisdom and the theories and methodologies of a handful of psychologists and business gurus.

This is no bad thing. Too much forensic prodding by scientists might undermine some of the worthwhile things that good coaching does and might even undermine notions of free will, self-responsibility and choice – the very cornerstones of the discipline. There is nothing remotely forensic about the best coaches: they are entirely human, quietly subversive and ready to challenge entrenched assumptions.

Using the power of lateral thinking techniques to give new perspectives to old problems, identifying core motivation, exploring people's real values, helping them come up with alternative courses of action, encouraging them to carry them through – all this is invaluable to those struggling with a world of bewildering complexity and change.

Having someone impartial to shine the mirror of reality or truth on you, whether in senior management or in life generally, is an exercise well worth embarking on. Socrates, who instinctively knew a thing or two about coaching techniques, was right when he said:

> Think not those faithful who praise all thy words and actions; but those who kindly reprove thy faults.

Bibliography

Block, P., 2nd edn, *Flawless Consulting: A Guide to Getting Your Expertise Used*, Jossey-Bass, 1999.

Block, P., 2nd edn, *Stewardship: Choosing Service Over Self-Interest*, Berrett-Koehler, 1996.

Boyzatis, R. and McKee, A., *Resonant Leadership: Renewing Yourself and Connecting with Others Through Mindfulness, Hope, and Compassion*, Harvard Business School Press, 2005.

Buckingham, M. and Clifton, D., *Now Discover Your Strengths: How to Develop Your Talents and Those of the People You Manage*, Simon & Schuster, 2001

Butler-Bowdon, T., *50 Self-help Classics: 50 Inspirational Books to Transform Your Life from Timeless Sages to Contemporary Gurus*, Nicholas Brealey, 2003.

Butler-Bowdon, T., *50 Psychology Classics: Who We Are, How We Think, What We Do*, Nicholas Brealey, 2006.

Clutterbuck, D., *Everyone Needs a Mentor: Fostering Talent in Your Organisation*, 4th edn, Chartered Institute of Personnel and Development, 2004.

Coffey, E., *10 Things That Keep CEOs Awake: And How to Put Them to Bed*, McGraw-Hill, 2002.

Colley, H., *Mentoring for Social Inclusion*, RoutledgeFalmer, 2003.

Covey, S., *The Eighth Habit: From Effectiveness to Greatness*, Free Press, 2005.

Covey, S., *The Seven Habits of Highly Effective People*, Simon & Schuster, 1989.

Csikszentmihalyi, M., *Creativity: Flow and the Psychology of Discovery and Invention*, HarperCollins, 1996.

Delves Broughton, P., *What They Teach You At Harvard Business School: My Two Years Inside the Cauldron of Capitalism*, Viking, 2008.

Dilts, R. and DeLozier, J., *The Encyclopedia of Systemic NLP & NLP New Coding*, NLP University Press, 2000.

Dixon, P., *Building a Better Business: The Key to Future Marketing, Management and Motivation*, Profile Books, 2005.

Ehrenreich, B., *Bait and Switch: The (Futile) Pursuit of the American Dream*, Metropolitan Books, 2005.

Ehrenreich, B., *Bright-sided: How the Relentless Promotion of Positive Thinking Has Undermined America*, Metropolitan Books, 2009.

Frankel, L., *Nice Girls Don't Get the Corner Office: 101 Unconscious Mistakes Women Make*, Little, Brown and Company, 2004.

Goldsmith, M., *What Got You Here Won't Get You There: How Successful People Become Even More Successful*, Hyperion Books, 2007.

Goleman, D., *Emotional Intelligence: Why It Can Matter More Than IQ*, Bloomsbury, 1995.

Goleman, D., *Working with Emotional Intelligence*, Bloomsbury, 1999.

Hindle, T., *Guide to Management Ideas and Gurus*, Profile Books, 2008.

Hooper, W. and Hooper, K., *The Puritan Gift: Triumph, Collapse and Revival of an American Dream*, I.B. Tauris & Co, 2008.

Jay, J., *Sack Your Boss!: Quit Your Job and Turn Your Passion into Your Profession*, Crown House Publishing, 2005.

Johnson, S. and Blanchard, K., *The One Minute Manager*, William Morrow, 1981.

Kaiser, R. (ed.), *The Perils of Accentuating the Positive*, Hogan Press, 2009.

Kellaway, L., *Martin Lukes: Who Moved My BlackBerry?*, Viking, 2005.

Levine, M., *The Price of Privilege : How Parental Pressure and Material Advantage Are Creating a Generation of Disconnected and Unhappy Kids*, HarperCollins, 2006.

MacDonald, M. and McKenna, P. (ed.), *The Power of Coaching... Engaging Excellence in Others!*, PLI Publishing, 2007.

McKenna, C., *The World's Newest Profession: Management Consulting in the Twentieth Century*, Cambridge University Press, 2006.

Peters, T. and Waterman, R., *In Search of Excellence: Lessons from America's Best-run Companies*, Harper & Row, New York, 1982; Profile Books, London, 2004.

Prahalad, C.K., *The Fortune at the Bottom of the Pyramid*, Wharton School Publishing, 2004.

Rosinski, P., *Coaching Across Cultures*, Nicholas Brealey Publishing, 2003.

Schein, E., *Career Dynamics: Matching Individual and Organizational Needs*, Addison-Wesley, 1978.

Schein, E., *Process Consultation: Its Role in Organization Development*, Addison-Wesley, 1969.

Seldon, A., *Blair Unbound*, Simon & Schuster, 2007.

Seligman, M., *Authentic Happiness: Using the New Positive Psychology to Realize Your Potential for Lasting Fulfillment*, Simon & Schuster, 2002.

Seligman, M., *The Optimistic Child*, Houghton Mifflin, 2007.

Senge, P., *The Fifth Discipline: The Art and Practice of The Learning Organisation*, Currency/Doubleday, New York, 1990; 2nd revised edn, Random House Business Books, 2006.

Weiss, A., *Million Dollar Consulting: The Professional's Guide to Growing a Practice*, 2nd edn, McGraw-Hill, 1997.

Whitmore, J., *Coaching for Performance: GROWing Human Potential and Purpose – the Principles and Practice of Coaching and Leadership*, 4th edn, Nicholas Brealey, 2009.

Wilber, K., *The Spectrum of Consciousness*, 2nd edn, Quest Books, 1996.

Index

group support 8
groups 8
GROW model 77–8
Grussing, Kate 152
gun crime 39
Guru Maharajah Ji 80

H
H&M 148
Haas Business School, UC Berkeley: *Opt-Out Patterns Across Careers: Labour Force Participation Rates Among Highly Educated Mothers* 145
Hagedown, Vince 44
happiness 13, 14, 20, 89, 206
classes 208–9
Harder & Company Community Research 121
Harnisch, Ruth Ann 95, 149–50
Harrigan, Kathryn 29
Harrison, John 194
Harrison, Roger 83
Harvard Business Review 5, 115, 131, 136
"The Realities of Executive Coaching" 63
"What Can Coaches Do for You?" 61
Harvard Business School (HBS) 37, 145, 157, 166
Harvard University 79, 119
Graduate School of Education 37
Harvey-Jones, John 166
Hay, Julie 83, 101, 107, 108
Hay Group 116
Hayes, Catherine 69, 169
Hayes, Laura 67
HBOS 166
health 13
health care 200–203
Health Professions Council (HPC) 99
Heart Chorus programme 90
Heidegger, Martin 28
"helicopter parenting" 208
Hemery, David 74
Henman, Tim 74
Hersey, Paul 21, 91
Hewitt Associates 164
hierarchy 47, 73, 132
Higgins, Monica 37
high power distance cultures 46
high-level coaches 65
Hill, Napoleon: *Think and Grow Rich* 28
hippie movement 6, 18
Hobbes, Thomas 9
Hofstede, Geert 46
Hogan, Robert 169

Homan, Madeline 96–7
Homer
The Iliad 36, 38
Odyssey 33
Hooper, William and Hooper, Kenneth: *The Puritan Gift* 165
Hornby, Andy 166
Horner, Caroline 99, 117
Hoskyns, John 42
hotel industry, coaching in the 124–40
HSBC 132–3, 134
human consciousness 17
human development 28, 105
human motivational theories 83
human potential movement 5, 6
human resources 64, 96, 131
human resources journals 5
humanistic movement 6
humanistic philosophy 75
humanistic psychology 17–18, 19, 77
humanistic-transpersonal school 11
Hussain, Zulfi 107
Hussein, Saddam 177
Hutton inquiry/report 177, 178
hypnotherapy 15

I
i-coach academy 99, 117, 134
IATA 59
Ibarra, Herminia 147
IBM 70, 76, 80, 87, 132
"Leaders in a Global Economy" survey (2003) 145
ICF *see* International Coach Federation
ICI 166
ideas 22
Imelt, Jeff 37, 150
imprint 13
India: survey of skills and competencies 168–9
Indian School of Management, Hyderabad 166
individualism 20
individuation of self 17
indoctrination 31
industrial psychologists 6
Industrial Revolution 45
industrialisation 46
industry standards 65, 132
inferiority complex 11
information
soliciting 32
withholding from colleagues 92
"informed forced consent" 211
"informers" 54, 65